U.S. STEAMSHIPS

A Picture Postcard History

by

FRANK O. BRAYNARD

Introduction by WALTER CRONKITE

ALMAR PRESS
BOOK PUBLISHERS

4105 Marietta Drive, Vestal NY 13850
(607) 722-0265 and 6251

DEDICATION

This book is dedicated to my wife Doris.

ACKNOWLEDGEMENTS

It is a pleasure to acknowledge the help in the proofreading of this book from the following people. They are Edward Hammond, friend and volunteer at the American Merchant Maine Museum, Stephen Rubenaker who assisted me for one year while a High School Senior at North Shore High School, Glen Head, NY, Harvey N. Roehl whose careful scrutiny of the text helped to create a better manuscript, and Dianna Weiner for her excellent editing of the page proofs.

I am also grateful to the publisher of Almar Press, for the initial suggestion for this work and his help throughout its creation. And finally a special word of thanks to Walter Cronkite for his Introduction to this book.

Library of Congress Cataloging-in-Publication Data

Braynard, Frank Osborn, 1916-
   U.S. steamships: a picture postcard history / by Frank O.
Braynard ; introduction by Walter Cronkite. — 1st ed.
   p. cm.
  Includes bibliographical references and index.
  ISBN 0-930256-15-8
  1. Steamboats in art. 2. Postcards — United States.
  3. Steamboats — United States — History. I. Title.
  NC1878.S4B73 1991
  741.6'83'0973 — dc20.

                         91-4409
                            CIP

Copyright © 1991 by ALMAR PRESS
                 4105 Marietta Drive
                 Vestal, New York 13850

First Edition, First Printing . . . . . . December 1991

PRINTED IN THE UNITED STATES OF AMERICA

INTRODUCTION

This unique book is a Picture Postcard history of American passenger carrying ships of all types, in all U.S. coastal areas. There are 220 illustrations of Postcards; many printed in the 19th Century, and some of which are quite rare. All are reproduced in actual size — in black and white — except those reproduced in color on the front and back covers of the book. All types of self-propelled ships are included: ferries, luxurious Great Lake passenger boats, excursion steamers, great white Fall River Line overnight boats, and a few trans-Atlantic liners. The Postcards are primarily photographs showing artist's conceptions, reproductions of paintings, and two are drawings by the author that were made into postcards. Each Post-card is accompanied by a caption with historical facts, technical information, and anecdotal material. All the Postcards are from the author's collection.

Frank Braynard has been writing about ships for most of his 74 years and has 37 other books and sketch portfolios to his credit. The reader of this book will be able to step back in time and see the evolution of U.S. Steamships from their beginning.

Left to right:
Frank O. Braynard and Walter Cronkite

Photo: J. Royal Parker

PREFACE

The popularity of U.S. Steamships and Postcard collecting provide an opportunity to create a book of lasting historical, artistic, and practical value. The opportunity to illustrate and describe the Postcards in a book was a challenging and educational event. I am certain that many important ships were not included; either as a result of the fact that Postcards were not produced to illustrate the ships or I have not been able to acquire the Postcards. Hopefully, the owners of these Postcards will place some of them into circulation.

The Postcard (or View as it is known to Postcard Collectors) has been previously described as a snapshot in time. Ordinarily it may represent a building, street, home, scenic wonder, specific event, or any other subject involving human endeavor at the moment the picture was taken or the painting or drawing was made. In this book the scenes are of ships and their related activities.

The Postcard was initially used as an inexpensive and rapid means of communication between people. Usually, on one side, there is a small space for a message, the address, postage stamp(s), and on the other side a photograph or other form of reproduction of the scene. The communication written on the Postcard may or may not be related to the scene. The writer may have used a Postcard showing a picture of a ship to inquire about the activities of another member of the family or a friend.

Over a period of many years the Postcards were collected for the message, history, and the scene. As a result of these collecting interests we have a valuable source of information relating to many subjects, including steamships, from a historical, technical, and artistic perspective. The Postcards shown in this book provide a chronological history of U.S. Steamships.

As indicated above, any collection of these steamship Postcards must be incomplete because of the limited availability of the Postcards. We are fortunate that people passed the collections to other members of their family and friends.

As a result, this book is a careful selection of the available scenes. In some instances, only one reproduction of a particular ship was available to this writer, although, other scenes must exist. The descriptive captions for each scene offer historical and technical information combined with the the comments of many interested people (see ACKNOWLEDGEMENTS and BIBLIOGRAPHY) and this writer. No claim is made to originality or completeness in the captions.

A NOTE TO THE DELTIOLIGISTS:

To provide reference information for your collection of these Postcards, the following information was taken from each Postcard and added below each illustration.

Publisher:	(Name and address of the publisher and Postcard No.)
Manufacturer:	(Name and Address)
Type:	(Chrome, Black and White, Artist Color, Real Photograph, Linen, etc.)
Postmark:	(If the Postcard has been used, name of the Town, State, and Date)
Value Index:	(A single letter based on the following code)

A	=	Very Rare
B	=	Rare
C	=	Fairly Rare
D	=	Scarce
E	=	Fairly Common
F	=	Common
G	=	Very Common

If any of these five items of information are not printed on either side of the Postcard then ``Not Indicated'' is shown below the illustration. There are listings that include all five items, some show one or more items, and some show none of the items.

CONNECTICUT'S FIRST STEAM VEHICLE

Publisher: Not Indicated • Manufacturer: Not Indicated • Glossy Photograph • Postmark: Not Used • Value Index: A

The application of steam power to boats has been described as America's major contribution to Western Civilization. Although John Fitch and Robert Fulton rightfully should be credited with the first practical steamboats put into commercial use, there were countless early efforts in the late Eighteenth Century in the United States. One of these is shown in this illustration. It is an artist's conception made based on the development of a paddle-wheel steamer built by Samuel Morey, who lived on the Upper Connecticut River in a town called Orford. He was so secretive during his early experimentation that he tested his first steamboat on a Sunday when everyone else was in church so that no one would see him. He is credited with building a craft that is reported to have succeeded in going upstream against the river's current, which was the purpose of all the effort. Later reports stated that he tested an improved design with engine and paddle wheel in the bow of the boat. The strange vehicle appears to have wheels as well as a paddle wheel. The original caption on the Postcard was "New England's First Steam Vehicle." Someone, a stickler for fact, changed this statement to "Connecticut's First Steam Vehicle."

The *SAVANNAH* of 1819 was described as a "Laudable and meritorious experiment to test the feasibility of the use of steam on the oceans of the world." Conceived by Captain Moses Rogers, the 98-foot long vessel was built in New York City, but owned by a group of Savannah, GA merchants. With an 80 horsepower engine, the 300-ton ship could steam at six knots without sails. The "Elegant steam ship," as newsmen

Publisher: Ships of the Sea Museum, Savannah, GA. • Manufacturer: Plastichrome, Boston, MA • Type: Colored Photograph • Postmark: Not Legible • Value Index: E

of the day described the SAVANNAH, sailed on her first and only trans-Atlantic voyage on May 22, now observed as National Maritime Day. The ship had two boilers with fire in them and no one dared to book passage aboard or to ship cargo on the steamer. The voyage was made in the hope that the vessel could be sold to a foreign buyer. The ship's 25 tons of coal and 50 cords of wood permitted Captain Rogers to steam for 105 hours on the 29-day trip to Liverpool, England. The Swedish King and the Czar of Russia offered to buy the ship based on barter arrangements. Captain Rogers could not accept these offers. The vessel returned to America and was converted into a sailing ship, operating successfully until 1821 when she ran aground.

1

The *WASHINGTON* of 1847 began regular trans-Atlantic service under the Stars and Stripes. Jointly subsidized by the United States and the city of Bremen, Germany, she was the first steamer to travel up the Weser River to Bremerhaven and the first American steamer in regular Atlantic service. Hailed by the *New York Herald* as "The most complete and beautiful" vessel ever built, the ship measured 1,700 tons and had a length of 260 feet. Her figurehead was President Washington. *The London Times*, with an anti-American bias, called her "About as ugly a specimen of steamship building" as they had

Publisher: The Author • Manufacturer: Stevenson Printers, Glen Cove, NY • Type: Sepia Tone Glossy Photograph • Postmark: Not Used • Value Index: F

ever seen. The welcome in Germany was enthusiastic. A bevy of flag-bedecked craft escorted the ship to a pier. A 6-foot model of the steamer was presented by the ship's officers to the City Fathers of Bremen, Germany and the Ocean Steam Navigation Company announced that the sistership would be named *HERMANN*, after a German hero. The *WASHINGTON*, which originally cost $390,000, was sold for $40,000 at a foreclosure sale in 1854. The ship was bought some time later by the famous Pacific Mail Line and was sold for scrap in 1864.

In 1857 Commodore Cornelius Vanderbilt built a huge new liner for the trans-Atlantic route. The ship was 331-feet long, had two tall smokestacks and cost the unheard-of sum of $800,000. The Commodore named the ship *VANDERBILT*. When the Civil War began, Vanderbilt was having a feud with the Navy, and he offered his newest liner to President Lincoln. He promised to strengthen the bow of the wooden-hulled craft with 50 feet of iron plating and to search for Confederate raiders, particularly the much-

Publisher: Nautical Photo Agency, London, England • Manufacturer: Not Indicated • Type: Glossy Photograph • Postmark: Not Used • Value Index: D

feared ironclad *MERRIMAC*. Vanderbilt asked to be placed in charge of the work and designated as the commander. President Lincoln acquiesced. The new ram bow was built, the steamer's wooden paddlewheel boxes were strengthened and 500 bales of cotton were stacked around the twin walking beams between her smokestacks. Two 100 pounders and twelve 9-inch guns were placed on board. The steamer was ready in seven days. The *MONITOR* located the *MERRIMAC* and the *VANDERBILT* steamed off in search of the dreaded British-built Confederate commerce raider *ALABAMA*. The *VANDERBILT* missed the *ALABAMA* by only a few hours off the Cape of Good Hope.

RIVER BOAT LOADED WITH COTTON BALES "AS IT USED TO BE"—X8

This illustration shows a stern-wheeled Mississippi River steamboat built in 1861 as the *CARONDELET*. She was initially designed as a naval *MONITOR*-type vessel. This configuration is a post-Civil War reconstruction. Her original name was retained. A sign written in large letters, states the craft was carrying a record load of 9,226 bales of cotton.

This boat had massive king posts at the bow and stern to which were attached guy wires fore and aft. These wires were kept taut to give longitudinal strength to the hull. One reason for

Publisher: E.C.Kropp Company, Milwaukee WI • Manufacturer: Not Indicated • Type: Color Dull Finish • Postmark: Sewickley, PA, July 5, 1948 • Value Index: D

the very tall smokestacks was to keep the sparks away from the highly flammable cotton and to permit good draft for the boilers as forced draft was not known at this stage of steam engine development. The small size of the people in the illustration indicates the large size of this boat. Her pilot house was five decks high and the stern wheel was at least 30 feet in diameter. After being rebuilt, the vessel was renamed the *CHARLES P. CHOUTEAH.*

It was June 30, 1870 at New Orleans, LA. Over 10,000 spectators crowded the waterfront for the race between the NATCHEZ, the champion speed queen of the Mississippi, and the *ROBT. E. LEE* (not ROBERT), the challenger. The event was news throughout the Western world. Several times a day the new trans-Atlantic cable would carry dispatches to England describing the four-day race for dissemination throughout Europe.

The course was the 1,200 miles from New Orleans to St. Louis. The captains of the two steamers were Captain Thomas P. Leathers of

RACE BETWEEN THE "NATCHEZ" AND THE "ROBERT E. LEE," NEW ORLEANS, LA.—165

Publisher: E.C. Kropp & Company, Milwaukee, WI • Manufacturer: Not Indicated • Type: Color Dull Finish • Postmark: New Orleans, LA, July 22, 1935 • Value Index: E

the *NATCHEZ* and Captain John W. Cannon aboard the *ROBT. E. LEE*. The *LEE* somehow managed to develop a four-minute lead at the start. The NATCHEZ was in a second position which she could not change. It was a grudge race between Captain Cannon, a Union veteran of the Civil War, and Captain Leathers, a dyed-in-the wool Confederate. So strong were his Southern feelings he refused to raise the Stars and Stripes on his steamers until l885.The positions of the two steamers were unchanged until they reached the area between Memphis, TN and Cairo, IL. It became foggy and the *NATCHEZ* ran aground. The *ROBT. E. LEE* steamed out of sight, reaching St. Louis on July 4, 3 days, 18 hours, and 14 minutes after the start, 33 minutes ahead of the record.

The Civil War virtually destroyed deep-sea shipping under the American flag. The one company which continued to operate until World War I was the American Line initially known as the Keystone Line. This service began in 1870 with the first four iron steamships built for trans-oceanic service in America. The 3,126-ton vessels were named *PENNSYLVANIA*, *INDIANA*, *ILLINOIS* and *OHIO*. This illustration features one of the posters used by the American Line. These ships carried 100 people in Cabin Class and 800 in steerage, together with some freight. The company is said never to have lost a

Publisher: Made In Sweden • Manufacturer: Berlings • Type: Color Dull Finish • Postmark: Swedish-Gnesta, April 20, 1979 • Value Index: C

bag of mail or a passenger, but they continually lost money because their foreign competition was subsidized. In 1877 President Grant began his world tour on the *INDIANA*. The first of the four to be lost was the *PENNSYLVANIA*, which burned near Chile in 1918. The last of the ships to end her career was the Army cargo ship *SUPPLY*, ex-*ILLINOIS*, quietly scrapped in 1928. Originally, the company had been supported by the Pennsylvania Railroad. Later it was acquired by J.P. Morgan and became the American Line, the beginning of Morgan's effort to win a monopoly of trans-Atlantic steamer travel. His ship combine was known as the International Mercantile Marine.

After the Hudson River route of Fulton's *CLERMONT*, the next American waterway on which steam appeared was Long Island Sound. Steamers traveling to New Haven, New London, CT, Newport, Providence, RI, Fall River, and New Bedford, MA, with links by stage to Boston were created almost overnight. From the earliest days the Long Island Sound overnight boats were elegant white-painted beauties. More than 50 years of steamboat development passed before the earliest Postcard showing Long Island Sound steamers became common. This Postcard shows the *RHODE ISLAND* built in 1873. Professor E. L.

Steamboat Landing, Stonington, Conn.

Publisher: G.A. Hyde, Stonington, CT, Card No. 973 • Manufacturer:Made In Germany • Type: Color Dull Finish • Postmark: Not Used • Value Index: E

Dunbaugh, of the Webb Institute calls the 312-foot steamer "The most interesting new steamer of the early 1870s and also one of the most beautiful ever to run on the Sound." She was built for the Stonington Line with a hog frame, the white structure curving over her port paddle wheel box. The hog frame was required to provide strength to the long wooden hull. The placement of the Dining Saloon on the Main deck is explained in Fred Dayton's book **STEAMBOAT DAYS** as allowing the diners to see through windows. She was wrecked in 1882.

Excursion Boat Warwick.

Publisher: R. Wilkinson, 55 Eddy St., Providence, RI • Manufacturer: V.H.C. Card No. 347 • Type: Color Dull Finish • Value Index E

The Providence, Fall River and Newport Steamboat Company put the little excursion boat DAY STAR (later WARWICK) into service in 1873. Built at Bull's Ferry, NJ, this 193-foot long steamer survived one serious fire and a sinking, ran under two different names and many different owners, and served for 62 years. This long service was an amazing life for a wooden vessel in that fast-changing era. The DAY STAR had a walking beam, a tall single smokestack, three masts with top masts attached, and forward and aft flag staffs almost as tall as the masts. This structure created a typical Sound steamer outline. Her tonnage was 681 tons gross. Gross tonnage was the standard way of measuring a ship's capacity, with 100 cubic feet equaling one gross ton (with many exceptions).

Records indicate that the DAY STAR carried more passengers out of Newport, RI than any other steamer. The ship was rebuilt as shown, and given a new name, WARWICK, and the doughty craft began a second career. In 1923 the steamer was sold for use as an East River excursion boat. During her career she regularly carried as many as 2,000 people per trip. She was scrapped in 1935 at Staten Island.

Publisher: E.F. Clements, San Francisco, CA • Manufacturer: Security Lithograph Company, San Francisco, CA • Type: Color Chrome • Postmark: Not Used • Value Index: E

This photograph shows one of the large San Francisco, CA ferry boats, the side-wheeler SACRAMENTO. Built in 1877, it served until recently and is approaching the Bay Bridge. For nearly a century ferries were the principal means for moving large numbers of commuters across the Bay at San Francisco. A large fleet of ferries was built for this service, initially for people and carriages and then for cars and the walking public. They were usually double enders, similar to this vessel. Notice how the wake starts as the paddle wheels cut the water and turn it to white foam and the twin pilot houses, common to all double enders. The SACRAMENTO was built in San Francisco. The size is evidence of how rapidly that port city had grown in less than three decades following the Gold Rush. The ferry measured 2,254 gross tons and had a length of 268 feet. This vessel was owned by the South Pacific Railway Company of California. The crew consisted of 18 men, according to the 1925 issue of **MERCHANT VESSELS**, annual publication of the U.S. Department of Commerce.

Guns were fired, sirens blown, and a great crowd was on hand when the *CITY OF RIO DE JANEIRO* was launched for the New York & Brazil Mail SS Company in March 1878, at Philadelphia, PA. John Roach knew the importance of publicity. He became famous for his introduction of iron as a replacement for wood in American shipbuilding. He launched the second of three new sisterships the, *CITY OF PARA*, as illustrated in this photograph. A 16-car Pullman train brought 600 dignitaries from Washington, including President Rutherford B. Hayes and his Cabinet. There was a crowd of 1,500 people.

Publisher: E.C.Kropp Company, Milwaukee WI • Manufacturer: Not Indicated • Type: Color Dull Finish • Postmark: Sewickley, PA, July 5, 1948 • Value Index: D

Each of the new ships could accommodate 100 passengers in First Class, 400 passengers in Steerage, plus 50,000 bags of coffee. Twenty days were required to travel to Rio de Janeiro, Brazil steaming at 14 knots. The *CITY OF PARA* measured 3,404 gross tons and had a length of 345 feet. The third ship was named *CITY OF PERNAMBUCO*. Two were sold in 1881 to Pacific Mail, the *CITY OF RIO DE JANEIRO* used in their trans-Pacific service and the *CITY OF PARA* in their Atlantic Line from New York to the Isthmus of Panama. Both of these steamers were acquired by the United States Government for service as troopships in the Spanish American War. The *CITY OF RIO DE JANEIRO* sank with the loss of 128 lives in 1901. The *CITY OF PARA* continued to operate until 1923 and was used between Panama and San Francisco, CA.

Two passenger ships were built in Chester, PA in 1879, and both were named *SANTIAGO*. One was for the Mallory Line and was immediately sold to Russia. The other, built for Ward Line, was in use until 1924, when she sank in a storm off Cape Hatteras, NC with the loss of 25 lives. This photograph shows the second *SANTIAGO* being unloaded at a pier. The steamer's black smokestack has two thin white bands for the Ward Line funnel markings. The ship had a length of 269 feet. The *SANTIAGO*'s speed was 13 knots using a single screw and a compound engine. The illustration

Publisher: E.C. Kropp & Company, Milwaukee, WI • Manufacturer: Not Indicated • Type: Color Dull Finish • Postmark: New Orleans, LA, July 22, 1935 • Value Index: E

shows the cargo-handling methods of the day, with her cargo booms out over the pier and her side port open. It is an excellent view of load-handling of an early American coastal steamer. The Ward Line became one of America's most important steamship companies.

6

State of Ohio.

Publisher: Illustrated Postal Card Company, New York, NY, Card No. 224-6 • Manufacturer: Made in Germany • Type: Color Glossy Photograph • Postmark: Not Used • Value Index: D

Steamships on the Great Lakes developed rapidly. By 1880, when the STATE OF OHIO was built, there had been 60 years of evolution which had produced a distinctive lake-type passenger ship design. The high forward section, straight stem and a promenade going far aft were developments in this design. In the next two decades ships with the same general appearance came into service with twice the tonnage.

The STATE OF OHIO was built for the Cleveland and Buffalo Transit Company at Wyandotte, MI. Instead of highlighting the paddle wheels with colorfully decorated paddle-wheel boxes, the company disguised the upper part of the hull covering the wheel by using the space as a huge nameboard. Only the wake along the waterline indicated the fact that a paddle wheel was working under the ship's outer skin. The massive crisscrossed timbers along the hull were located to fend the ship off the pier and prevent damage to the hull. The STATE OF OHIO measured 1,221 gross tons and the hull was 225 feet long. The steamer had a career lasting 44 years and never had a serious accident. On May 20, 1924, while at the pier at Cleveland, the fine old vessel was destroyed by fire.

Publisher: Not Indicated • Manufacturer: Not Indicated • Type: Photograph • Postmark: Not Used • Value Index: D

The coast of Maine rapidly came to be the scene of extensive steamboat activity with many of the local craft built for specialized services. One of the largest, the STATE OF MAINE, is shown in this illustration. The ship's length was 156 feet. The 714-gross-ton steamer was built in 1882 at Wilmington, DE. In 1904 the Joy Line bought the STATE OF MAINE and renamed her LARCHMONT, a name that Professor E. Dunbaugh said in his book **THE ERA OF THE JOY LINE**, was picked to rhyme with EDGEMONT, the regular Joy Line steamer of that day.

The LARCHMONT had twin smokestacks, the EDGEMONT had only one. The LARCHMONT had masts rigged for sails, while the EDGEMONT did not have masts. Both ships had handsome paddle-box decorations. When the Joy Line service ended, the EDGEMONT was laid up in Philadelphia, PA. In 1916, the ship was renamed CAPE MAY, as shown in the illustration, and was used as a day excursion boat. During America's participation in World War I, the ancient vessel became a barracks ship for a wartime shipyard in Bristol, PA. The ship was returned after the war to Philadelphia for more idleness. On September 24, 1925, the old lady was burned for the scrap metal in the hull.

The *ATLANTIC CITY* was ahead of her time. Contructed as an "All steel steamship" the Atlantic City Steamship Line was very proud of this fact, using the phrase in their advertising. The ship used pole masts, different from the traditional sailing ship mast design. Although the ship was small it was decidedly modern in 1883 when built at Wilmington, DE. The vessel measured 422 gross tons and the hull was 145 feet in length. The *ATLANTIC CITY* Postcard featured a painting of the steamer at sea. From the height of the waves the vessel would have been rolling quite a

A SAIL On The Sea In a Real OCEAN STEAM SHIP

Publisher: Atlantic City SS Line • Manufacturer: Not Indicated • Type: Black-White Dull Finish • Postmark: Not Used • Value Index: C

bit in actual sea conditions; however, the company wanted the ship to look steady and serene, so the artist made the painting that way. The message on the back reads "The All Steel Steamship *ATLANTIC CITY* Leaves For a Two Hour Ride On The Ocean Head of North New Jersey Ave. Every Sunday at 3 P.M. Fare 50c Children 25 c. Atlantic City Steamship Line Bell Phone 3241. Coast 757." In later years the steamer was operated by the Delaware River Ferry Company of New Jersey.

This vessel was a true steamship with pole masts and no evidence of sails. Built in 1885 at Chester, PA., the *COMAL* set the design mode for countless American coastal passenger ships for the next one-half century. The low smokestack makes her look modern. In the years that followed, naval architects would experiment with taller and taller stacks. When the concept of forced draft was perfected the stacks would, for a time, become shorter. The COMAL was owned by the Mallory Steamship Company. The Mallory Line made its reputation after the Civil War on the run from New York City to Galveston, TX. Their

Comal

MALLORY STEAMSHIP COMPANY

The Direct Passenger and Fast Freight "Ocean Route" from and to Texas and the Southwest

Galveston, Tex.   Mobile, Ala.   Tampa, Fla.   Key West, Fla.   New York

Publisher: Not Indicated • Manufacturer: Not Indicated • Type: Black-White Dull Finish • Postmark: Not Used • Value Index: E

motto was "The direct Passenger and Fast Freight 'Ocean Route' From and To Texas and the Southwest." The clean sweep of the COMAL deck line, uninterrupted from bow to the stern, was distinctive and appealing, as was the rake to the single thick stack. The pilot house was not on the main deck, as in earlier coastal steamers, but had been raised to the top deck. This was a wise step for a ship of over 300 feet in length. The *COMAL* measured 2,934 gross tons. The ship was driven by an engine of 1,900 horsepower.

The steamship *ALLIANCA* belonging to the Panama Rail Road Steamship Line is shown in 1914 entering Gatun Locks at the Panama Canal as one of the first steamers to transit the new Canal. The line was a United States Government-owned operation which continued to serve the needs of those who worked at the Canal for another 50 years. The *ALLIANCA* was built in 1886 and was a typical Chester-built iron steamer of the time period. The ship was 295 feet long. Note the new-style patent anchors on either side of the bow, eliminating the age-old custom of having the anchor on the foredeck,

Panama Rail Road Steamer entering Gatun Locks, Panama Canal

Publisher: Not Indicated • Manufacturer: Not Indicated • Type: Photograph • Postmark: Not Used • Value Index: C

with its chain looping down to the hawse pipe opening. This anchor was drawn tightly into the hawse hole and usually remained snug and safe. To compare the designs see the difference between the *CITY OF PARA*'s anchor chain and this new concept.

With 3,500 horsepower the ship was fast at that time. Note the numerous cargo booms on the fore and main masts, the *ALLIANCA* also carried cargo in addition to passengers.

This illustration is of the 1886 flagship of the Detroit & Cleveland Line, a strong competitor of the Cleveland & Buffalo Transit Company. The ship is the *CITY OF ST. IGNACE*, built at Wyandotte, MI. The basic style, green-painted hull, gold name letters, and stacks, arranged side by side, shows a vessel much the same as the *STATE OF OHIO*. The steamer measured 1,923 gross tons and had a length of 272 feet. In appearance the main difference between the *CITY OF ST. IGNACE* and the *STATE OF OHIO* was the passenger deck above the top of the paddle wheel boxes.

Despite the fact that

D. & C. Express Steamer, City of St. Ignace.

Publisher: Illustrated Postal Card Company, New York, NY, Card No. 224-2 • Manufacturer: Made In Germany • Type: Color Glossy • Postmark: Not Used • Value Index: D

ships of this day had superstructures built entirely of wood, most of them seemed to live charmed lives by escaping destructive fires. The *CITY OF ST. IGNACE* was listed in a company brochure of 1921. She was then the oldest and smallest in a fleet of eight ships. Passenger ships on the Great Lakes carried travelers in first class luxury. They also carried large numbers of immigrants that were heading to the West. For these people there were dormitories on the lower decks. However, carrying immigrants was very important as they made a profit for most Great Lake ship lines.

Steamer "NANTUCKET".   2004

Publisher: A.C. Bosselman & Company, New York, NY • Manufacturer: Made In Germany • Type: Color Photograph • Postmark: Not Used • Value Index: D

This Illustration shows the Martha's Vineyard ferry *NANTUCKET*. These large and fine the ferries were on the run between New Bedford, Woods Hole, Martha's Vineyard, MA, and Nantucket, RI. The *NANTUCKET* was a good example of old-style ferry design. The open bow deck was used to permit greater space for maneuvering and storing wagons and carts. The two covered passenger decks included space for staterooms.

S/S China

Publisher: Steamship Historical Society of America • Manufacturer: Not Indicated • Type: Black-White Photograph • Postmark: Not Used • Value Index: E

Ocean liner services on the Pacific lagged behind the Atlantic Ocean. The Pacific Mail Line's *COLORADO* began regular trans-Pacific passenger steamship operation under the American flag on January 1, 1867. By 1889 the company built a ship of a style that had never been seen on the Pacific. The new ship was named CHINA and was more than twice the size of the *COLORADO*. The *CHINA* was built in Govan, Scotland, by the Fairfield Shipbuilding & Engineering Company. The new ship measured 5,060 gross tons and a length of 440 feet. All early Pacific Mail vessels had square sails and used them. The *CHINA*'s configuration was almost modern with four tall pole masts (one-piece masts with no break halfway up for a top mast to be added) and two large funnels. The ship's black steel hull and a forward bridge and pilot house added to the modern look.

These illustrations show how this ship's silhouette was drastically altered. Both Postcards show the same vessel, the *CITY OF NEW YORK*, built in 1888. The illustration above shows the ship as originally built; the illustration below shows the liner after rebuilding and renamed the *NEW YORK*. This historic vessel and a sister-

Publisher: Universal Postal Card Company, New York, NY • Manufacturer: Not Indicated • Type: Colored Photograph •. Postmark: Not Used • Value Index: D

ship, the *CITY OF PARIS* (renamed *PHILADELPHIA*), were the last of a famous line of trans-Atlantic steamships built for the Inman Line. They were the first major Atlantic passenger liners designed to have twin screw propulsion. This design was important in liner history as a guarantee that sails would not have to be used to reach home if the propeller shaft broke. Despite this feature, the two liners originally had sails and used them.

The twin ships were especially important to America when sold to J. P. Morgan in 1893 for his International Mercantile Marine (IMM). The external changes made in the IMM ships hurt their appearance. The middle smokestack was removed and the other two smokestacks were increased in height for better draft. They were among the last ships to have a curved clipper bow and bowsprit, similar to the forward configuration of sailing ships. Both were built by J. & G. Thompson, Ltd., of Clydebank, Glasgow, Scotland, they each measured 10,500 gross tons, 560 feet in length, of steel. Both held the coveted Blue Ribbon of the Atlantic, mythical emblem of speed supremacy. During

the Spanish American War the *NEW YORK* was renamed *HARVARD* and served as an armed auxiliary cruiser. In World War I, the aging vessel was again renamed *NEW YORK* and became a troopship. After that conflict the *NEW YORK* was laid up. In 1921 a Polish company bought the once-proud steamer. The company failed and the ship was scrapped in Genoa in 1923.

Publisher: Not Indicated • Manufacturer: Not Indicated • Type: Photograph Set Into Painting of a Sea • Postmark: Not Used • Value Index: E

There have been three Long Island Sound passenger steamers named *CONNECTICUT*. The first was designed by Robert Fulton for trans-Atlantic service. When Fulton died the ship was put into operation on overnight service on the Sound. The second, built in 1848, ran between New York City and Norwich, CT. This steamer became a northern transport during the Civil War, surviving in government service until the 1890s. The third was a 353-foot vessel built in 1889 for the New York to Providence Line. This ship is shown in this illustration. Although a very handsome steamer, this great ship was outmoded before she was completed because of

Steamer "Connecticut" at Landing, Stonington, Conn.

Publisher: G.A. Hyde, Stonington, CT, Card No. 987 • Manufacturer: Made in Germany • Type: Colored Photograph • Postmark: Not Used • Value Index: E

wooden construction. Other Sound steamers of this date were made of iron. However, the *CONNECTICUT* was an imposing craft with a towering paddle wheel box on either side rising four decks high and brightly gilded. The design was characteristic of all Long Island Sound steamers with a narrow hull, only 48 feet wide, on top of which was built a superstructure 87 feet wide. The overhang was supported by struts. The ship measured 3,399 gross tons, was built at Noank, CT, and became the flagship of the Providence & Stonington SS Company. In 1909 this steamer was laid up and then scrapped.

The *MANDALAY* built in 1889, was a commodious and somewhat awkward-looking day excursion steamer. The ship was built at Wilmington, DE, and was first given the name *EXPRESS*. The name did not fit as the vessel was not fast. However, the steamer was comfortable and had a career stretching over 40 years. The craft was hit and sunk by a large cargo ship in New York City Harbor near the Battery. The *MANDALAY* measured 1,120 gross tons and a length of 272 feet. The steamer was built for the Delaware and Hudson SS Company of Delaware. The crew was only 23 persons for 2,000 passengers. The

MANDALAY, ATLANTIC HIGHLANDS, N. J.

Publisher: Tichnor Quality Views-UNCO • Manufacturer: Not Indicated • Type: Colored Photograph • Postmark: Not Used • Value Index: E

MANDALAY was a propeller-driven steamer. The 10 banks of slits on the paddle-wheel box below the gold lettering of the steamer's name were designed for water to spurt out as the great wheel churned around. When iron or steel hulls replaced wooden construction the great hog frame, shown here just forward of the walking beam, was no longer required. Wooden hulls required this heavy truss to keep the hull from sagging at its ends.

The KENNEBEC, shown to the right in the illustration and her principal cabin, featured in the circular photo at the top, was built in Bath, ME. by the New England Ship Building Company in 1889. The Kennebec Steamship Company of Boston, MA, operated the steamer on various overnight routes out of Maine. The ship measured 1,652 gross tons and a length of 256 feet. The vessel's two masts, with top masts, were fitted with sails. The KEN-NEBEC had the old-style anchor arrangement at the stem. The smaller steamer to the left in the illustration was the

Publisher: Not Indicated • Manufacturer: Not Indicated • Type: Blac-White Photograph • Postmark: Not Used • Value Index: E

much older STAR OF THE EAST, built in 1866, later rebuilt, and given the new name SAGADOHOC in 1889. In later years this vessel was again renamed, becoming the GREENPORT. The KENNEBEC retained the same name serving on a variety of routes until 1912 when the name was changed to IROQUOIS. In 1924 the old steamer was scrapped.

The famous Merchants & Miners Line had a large fleet of steamers operating between Boston, MA and Baltimore, MD. The company began operations in 1855 with a unique ship naming system. Each ship was named for a county in either Massachusetts, Maryland or Virginia. The goal, or so it appeared, was to have one ship's name beginning with each letter of the alphabet. The company came close to accomplishing this effort with ALLEGHANY, BERKSHIRE, CHATHAM, DORCHESTER, ESSEX, and FAIRFAX for first six ships in their fleet in the days before World War I. The fleet reached the letter "T" at that time.

Publisher: Steamship Historical Society of America • Manufacturer: Not Indicated • Type: Black-White Photograph • Postmark: Not Used • Value Index: E

This illustration shows the ESSEX. Note the well-designed stack and pilot house. This steamship measured 3,018 gross tons, had a length of 295 feet and 2,000 horsepower. Built by William Cramp in 1890 at Philadelphia, PA, the ESSEX had sails and frequently used them. In 1906 the sleek hull was cut in half and lengthened with a new mid-section 25 feet long. Such drastic surgery happened quite frequently and often resulted in greater speed with lower fuel consumption. Unfortunately the ESSEX was lost off Block Island on September 26, 1941, at 51 years of age.

STEAMER "SANDY HOOK"   7472

Publisher: Atlantic Highlands Reproduction: Series 1 • Manufacturer: Not Indicated • Type: Reprint of Photograph •
Postmark: Red Bank, NJ, June 30, 1986 • Value Index: G

These two illustrations provide a fine example of how an old ship can be given a completely new lease on life by a good naval architect. The ship is the old flyer *SANDY HOOK*, built in 1889. The upper Postcard was published by the Atlantic Highlands Historical Society. The lack of sharp detail in the Postcard indicates it is a copy of an earlier photograph. The steamer was built at Wilmington, DE, for the Central Railroad of New Jersey. The *SANDY HOOK* measured 1,559 gross tons and had a length of 260 feet. The ship was driven by 3,200 horsepower, and was intended to rush New York City executives to their offices and then return them to their homes in New Jersey.

The good-looking, two-stacked vessel was taken over in 1932 by the naval architect George Sharp for a complete rebuilding. The transformation is shown in the lower illustration, with the steamer passing the lower part of New York City, outward bound. The ship's pilot house was raised a full deck to make room for a forward lounge with numerous windows overlooking the bow. Two finely proportioned new smokestacks and short, sharply raked masts completed the new silhouette.

Publisher: Not Indicated • Manufacturer: Not Indicated • Type: Black-White Photograph • Postmark: Not Used • Value
Index: E

An American coastal line which emerged in the days before the Civil War is particularly noteworthy. In poetry and song the legend of the Old Fall River Line has become a part of our national tradition. Fall River, MA offered the shortest water and rail route between New York City and Boston, MA. The first steamer of this line to win world fame was their *METROPOLIS* of 1855. A claim was made that this vessel was the largest and fastest steamer in the world at that date.

This illustration shows the *PLYMOUTH* of 1870. While slightly shorter than the METROPOLIS, this overnight vessel measured 3,770 gross tons, had

Publisher: Not Indicated • Manufacturer: Not Indicated • Type: Black-White Photograph • Postmark: Not Used • Value Index: E

five decks, and could make 20 knots with 5,500 horsepower. There was a walking beam carefully hidden in a cabin-like structure on the same level as the tall pilot house. The 325-foot long steamer is coming down the East River early in the morning, having passed under the Brooklyn Bridge heading toward the company terminal on the Hudson River side of lower Manhattan. Many of her 1,000 or more passengers may be comfortably sleeping at this time. Among the nautical firsts credited to the foresight of the Fall River Line was the use of fire sprinklers, a safety feature which put the company far ahead of all other ship lines in the world.

Gay Head, MA, on Martha's Vineyard is the western tip of that island. One of the most famous of all Martha's Vineyard's early steam ferries was named for this important location. The *GAY HEAD* was built in 1891 at Philadelphia, PA. From the tall flag pole far forward to the wide sponsons (struts) supporting the wide superstructure built out over the narrow hull, the ship was a handsome vessel. Typical of the designer's pride in his work was the gilded eagle that may be seen in this illustration on top of the pole rising in front of the pilot house. The pole replaced the old hog frame technique in

STR. GAY HEAD, NEW BEDFORD, MARTHA'S VINEYARD AND NANTUCKET STEAMBOAT LINE.

Publisher: W.A. Harding & Company, Oak Bluffs, MA • Manufacturer: C.T. American Art • Type Colored Dull Finish Photograph • Postmark: Not Used • Value Index: E

construction. One taut cable stretched to the bow and two others bracketed the smokestack, keeping the bow from sagging. A similar pole with three cables rose aft of the stack, providing longitudinal strength to the ship's stern. The after pole was capped with a gilded ball. The GAY HEAD measured 701 gross tons and had a length of 203 feet. After a long and uneventful career the old ferry was sold in 1924 to a New Yorker and renamed *PASTIME*. In 1931, the 40-year old steamer was burned to reclaim her metal.

THE GENERAL SLOCUM

© SLOCUM MEMORIAL COMMITTEE
THE QUEENS HISTORICAL SOCIETY 1975

The *GENERAL SLOCUM* caught fire on June 15, 1904, while approaching the dangerous Hell Gate, the narrow point where Manhattan's East River becomes Long Island Sound. Captain William Van Schaick, her Master, pressed ahead, fearful of the rocks and whirlpools that gave the passage the name. By the time he had beached her on North Brother Island she was an inferno. The fire and panic caused 1,021 of the 1,331 people aboard to die. Most were children on a Sunday school outing. America learned a

Publisher: Slocum Memorial Committee • Manufacturer: Raum Printing, Philadelphia, PA, Card No. 19140 • Black-White Glossy Photograph • Postmark: Not Used • Value Index: F

tragic lesson which resulted in the nation's inland waterway passenger boats being subject to the world's strictest fire safety regulations.

Built in 1891 in Brooklyn, NY, at the yard of John E. Hoffmire, the *GENERAL SLOCUM* was a wooden steamer measuring 1,284 gross tons and had a length of 250 feet. The public outcry after the disaster was so extensive that Captain Van Schaick was tried, found guilty of manslaughter, and sentenced to 10 years in prison. A number of maritime unions obtained petitions with 245,000 signatures to win a pardon for him. After he had served 3 years and 8 months, he was pardoned by President William H. Taft.

COLONIAL NAVIGATION COMPANY

BETWEEN NEW YORK AND NEW ENGLAND

The 246-foot sister-ships *WASHINGTON* and *NORFOLK* were built in 1891 for use on Chesapeake Bay. Constructed at Wilmington, DE, they were operated by the Norfolk & Washington Steamboat Company between Norfolk, VA and Washington, DC. In 1910 they were sold to the Colonial Line and renamed *LEXINGTON* (ex-*WASHINGTON*) and *CONCORD* to run between Providence, RI and New York City.

The *LEXINGTON* was hit by the freighter JANE CHRISTIANSON on January 2, 1935, while passing around the Battery, NY. The

Publisher: Colonial Line • Manufacturer: Not Indicated • Type: Colored Artist Conception • Postmark: Not Used • Value Index: F

overnight boat sank, four of her crew were lost, and the steamer was wrecked beyond repair.

All aboard for Yale-Harvard Boat Race. Steamer Richard Peck, New Haven, Conn.

Publisher: A.H.A.P. Company, New York, NY • Manufacturer: Made In Germany • Type: Colored Dull Finish Photograph • Postmark: Not Used • Value Index: E

The *RICHARD PECK*, built in 1892 at Wilmington, DE, measured 2,906 gross tons and was 303 feet in length. Using 3,500 horsepower, the Long Island Sound overnight boat was able to reach 20 knots and was one of the fastest in that service. Mr. A. Carey Smith was the naval architect. She was named in honor of the superintendent of the New Haven Line. A report on her interior :

"The elegance of the *PECK*'s decor in one item: the German Renaissance electric-lighting fixtures in the Main Saloon. These steel brackets were made to resemble a mythical medieval fire-spitting griffin. From the bird's mouth protruded an incandescent light with additional lights on either side of its outstretched wings."

The *RICHARD PECK* served between 1892 to 1900 on the New Haven Line, from 1900 to 1937 for the New England SS Company, and from 1937 to 1941 on the Mesick Line run. In 1938 the ship was chartered to Colonial Lines. Finally, in 1941 the Navy took the *RICHARD PECK* for World War II work. Purchased after the war by the Pennsylvania Railroad, the steamer was renamed *ELISHA LEE* and put on her last run for the ferry service.

The *CHRISTOPHER COLUMBUS*, built in 1892, was credited with carrying more passengers than any other steamer on the Great Lakes. The ship was designed by Captain Alexander McDougall, naval architect of Great Lakes fame. They were known as whalebacks because of their rounded hull and pig-nosed bow. The big craft was named in honor of Christopher Columbus and was initially used to take visitors to the Worlds Fair at Chicago, IL, for the 400th anniversary of the voyage of discovery.

When built at Superior, WI, the steamer did not have the top deck shown in the

Publisher: Max Rigot Selling Company, Chicago, IL, Card No. 420 • Manufacturer: C.T. American Art • Type: Colored Dull Finish Photograph • Postmark: Not Used • Value Index: E

illustration. As the ship was rebuilt to accommodate more people, she was given a large upper deck which increased her day passenger capacity to 5,000. The ship measured 1,511 gross tons and was 362 feet in length. Most of the steamer's life was spent on the service between Chicago, IL and Milwaukee, WI, a 170-mile run. Her 5,000 horsepower provided a speed of 18 knots. This vessel was scrapped in 1936 at Manitowoc, WI. The whistle was saved and installed as a part of that city's air raid warning system. The ship was elected in 1987 to the National Maritime Hall of Fame of the American Merchants Marine Museum, at Kings Point, NY.

Built in 1893, the *CITY OF ALPENA* II was one of the most famous steamers of the early Detroit and Cleveland Navigation Co. fleet. The ship was built in Wyandotte, MI and measured 1,919 gross tons with a length of 286 feet. The 2,000 horsepower engine was fitted with twin boilers having a steam pressure of 120 pounds-per-square-inch (PSI). This pressure was a large improvement over the 10 PSI available on the *SAVANNAH* of 1819, but primitive by today's standards. The company had two basic overnight services; one route from Detroit, MI to Cleveland, OH and the second from Detroit, MI to Buffalo, NY.

Publisher: Illustrated Postal Card Company, New York, NY, Card No. 224-7 • Manufacturer: Made In Germany • Type: Colored Dull Finish Photgraph • Postmark: Not Used • Value Index: E

The company literature of the period promised "A refreshing night's sleep and a timely arrival for a full day's business."

This illustration shows the Merchants & Miners Line's *GLOUCESTER*, built by the Maryland Steel Company at Sparrows Point, MD in 1893. This steamship was intended for ocean travel. The top masts and sails are not shown although they were carried and occasionally set. The vessel used a clean-cut, American-style hull and low superstructure so the ship would not roll in heavy seas. There was evidence of old style design such as the bow davit and deck-stowed anchors with chain looping down to the hawse pipe. The ship had the low pilot house. On either side was a

Publisher: Steamship Historical Society of America • Manufacturer: Not Indicated • Type: Black-White Glossy Photograph • Postmark: Not Used • Value Index: F

bridge for the officer of the deck to use for a better view when docking or undocking. A few years later the pilot house was raised and became the center part of this bridge on newer ships.

The *GLOUCESTER* measured 2,541 gross tons, was 272 feet long, with a beam of 42 feet. This steamship ran from Boston, MA to Philadelphia, PA except during the Spanish American and First World War 1 periods when it was used as a troopship. The *GLOUCESTER* was scrapped in 1938. The ship's "Blue Peter" or "Jack" flying at the bow, indicates a sailing day. It was lowered the moment the lines were let go and the ship moved out.

This illustration is taken from a Postcard, which reproduced a poor photograph made from an old glass negative, showing the Boston & Bangor Steamship Company's steamer *CITY OF BANGOR*. The ship was built at Bath, ME in 1894 and was the flagship of one of several small steamer lines eventually absorbed by the Eastern Steamship Company. The reader may ask why there was a little cabin with four windows and a door fitted aft of the twin smokestacks? It was a dummy cabin used to hide the walking beam which had become old fashioned in appearance. At the same time the ship

Publisher: Not Indicated • Manufacturer: Not Indicated • Type: Poor Reprint Glossy Photograph • Postmark: Not Used • Value Index: F

had the tall fore and main masts previously abandoned by most coastal steamers. Only four lifeboats can be seen on the ship, not sufficient for all passengers and crew and suggesting that the photograph predates the loss of the *TITANIC* in 1912.

The *NORTH WEST* and a sistership, the *NORTH LAND*, were two of the most luxurious passengers ships ever built for the American Merchant Marine. They were the product of the railroad genius, James J. Hill. This illustration shows the *NORTH WEST* as she first appeared with three smokestacks, one passenger deck above her hull, and a huge name pennant. The ship was built in 1894 by the Globe Iron Works of Cleveland, OH, at a cost of $650,000. The *NORTH WEST* was 386 feet long, a width of 44 feet, and measured 4,244 gross tons. The ship ran between Buffalo, NY and Duluth,

STEAMER "NORTH WEST." 1861

Publisher: A.C. Bosselman & Company, New York, NY • Manufacturer: Made In Germany • Type: Colored Artist Conception • Postmark: Not Used • Value Index: D

MN. The initial construction included accommodations for 350 persons in First Class and 300 persons in Second Class. The ship lost money in operation and the addition of more passenger space failed to help. In 1911 the *NORTH WEST* burned at the pier. In 1918, after years of idleness the steamer was cut in half to permit towing out of the Great Lakes for use in the Atlantic Ocean. En route the forward part sank in a storm on Lake Ontario. When the stern section reached Quebec it was joined to a new bow and named *MAPLECOURT*. Later, this ship was cut in half and moved back to the Great Lakes, reassembled and served for years as a freighter. In World War II the ship was torpedoed and sank in the Atlantic Ocean.

The *PRISCILLA* has been thought of as having the finest appearance of all Long Island Sound steamers. Built at Chester, PA in 1894, the big vessel measured 5,292 gross tons, was 440 feet long, and 52 feet wide. The *PRISCILLA* cost $1,500,000 to build and had 361 staterooms plus additional bunks to sleep 1,500 persons. The grand saloon was said to be the largest room afloat at the time, measuring 142 feet in length, 30 feet in width, and 24 feet in height. The *PRISCILLA*, with 56 watertight bulkheads, was one of the safest ships ever built. The only serious accident for this Fall River Line

7366 STR PRISCILLA. FALL RIVER LINE.

Providence, R.I. 4/28/12
Having a fine trip. Was rather rough last night at point Judith. Saw the "Commonwealth". She is a beauty. Best wishes, Fred

Publisher: Detroit Photographic Company-1901, Card No. 7366 • Manufacturer: Not Indicated • Type: Colored Dull Finish Photograph • Postmark: Providence, RI, April 28, 1912 • Value Index D

steamer occurred in 1902 during a dense fog when the steamship *POWHATAN* nearly cut off the bow, severing it almost to the keel. The forward watertight bulkhead prevented the ship from sinking. Twenty-two years later the *PRISCILLA* was the heroine in a rescue, removing 480 passengers from the *BOSTON*, a new competitor, after that ship had been struck in fog by the tanker *SWIFT ARROW*. After the PRISCILLA was scrapped in 1938 the whistle was removed and installed on a Jamestown to Newport, RI ferry.

This illustration shows the two-stacked *MIAMI*, owned by the small American company called the Peninsular and Occidental Steamship Company. This firm knowingly copied the name of the famous British ship line called the Peninsular and Oriental Line (Known today as P & O). The United States company operated a line of small steamers linking Florida and Cuba. The *MIAMI* had began life as the *GORDON ROWE*, and had been built in 1897 in Philadelphia, PA. With only 1,741 gross tonnage, the steamer had a length of 239 feet and a beam of 40 feet. The MIAMI had a crew of 50

S. S. MIAMI.

Publisher: Novelty Company of America • Manufacturer: Made In Germany • Type: Colored Dull Finish Photograph • Postmark: Not Used • Value Index: E

persons. Speed was not essential on the run and the ship's 205 horsepower allowed a leisurely voyage to Cuba. The MIAMI had a handsome, imposing outline. The main deck was entirely for cargo, as suggested by the two open side ports visible in the illustration. The cabins located on the upper deck aft were reserved by wealthy tobacco or sugar plantation owners seeking privacy. The bridge itself looks like an afterthought.

While the *ST. LOUIS* gave some Americans a brief feeling that there might be a maritime revival for the American flag on the North Atlantic, our coastal shipping continued to expand and evolve without fanfare. In 1896 the Plant Line built a handsome new passenger ship at Newport News, VA, the *LA GRANDE DUCHESSE.*

The new steamer's name set the vessel apart from other coastal liners. The name was French and it had been selected to honor the French citizens of Nova Scotia, Canada as the ship linked Boston, MA to Nova Scotia. The ship was

THE NEW YORK AND PORTO RICO STEAMSHIP CO.

Publisher: A.C.Bosselman & Company, New York, NY • Manufacturer:Made In Germany • Type: Colored Artist Conception • Postmark: Coamo, PR, June 10, 1907 • Value Index: D

both large and fast, with a 5,108 gross tonnage, a length of 381 feet, a beam of 47 feet, and speed of 15 knots. Look very closely, just forward of the main mast and note a glass dome over the smoking room aft. A special feature was the telephone in every cabin, a luxury for a coastal passenger vessel. She was later renamed the *CAROLINA*, as shown in the illustration.

This illustration shows the steamer *PARK CITY*, one of the relatively few ships which retained the same name throughout a long career. This handsome little steamer was known for style and design as shown in the retention of the golden eagle atop the rounded pilot house. Also note the rounded tops for the four forward pilot house windows suggesting a better class ship. The *PARK CITY* spent many years on the home port Bridgeport, CT to Port Jefferson, NY passenger car ferry run. Built in 1898 the *PARK CITY*'s dimensions were: a length of 143 feet, a beam of 28 feet, a draft of 9.9 feet, and measured 391 gross tons.

Steamer "Park City" from Bridgeport   Port Jefferson, Long Island, N. Y.

Publisher: Kane's Pharmacy, Port Ferrerson, NY • Manufacturer: The Albertype Company, Brooklyn, NY • Type: Black-White Dull Finish Photograph • Postmark: Not Used • Value Index: E

However, the steamer's design was that of a little liner and she could have crossed the Atlantic Ocean. In the Long Island Sound ferry service the ship had a crew of seven people. The vessel was a part of the McAllister fleet, a company known in recent years as the McAllister Brothers Towing Company operation in New York Harbor. The ship served 60 years.

Steamship St. Croix, Eastern S. S. Co.
Published in Germany for G. W. Morris, Portland, Maine.

Publisher: G.W. Morris, Portland, ME • Manufacturer: Made In Germany • Type: Colored Dull Finish Photograph • Postmark: Not Used • Value Index: E

AMERICAN LINE
NEW YORK AND SOUTHAMPTON.

S.S. ST. LOUIS
S.S. ST. PAUL / PASSING THE NEEDLES
NEAR SOUTHAMPTON.

Publisher: Not Indicated • Manufacturer: American Litho Company, New York, NY • Type: Colored Artist Conception • Postmark: Not Used • Value Index: D

The *ST. CROIX*, built in 1895 by the New England Steamboat Company, Bath, ME was owned by the International Steamship Company, a subsidiary of the Eastern Steamship Company. The steamer *ST. CROIX* had a length of 240 feet and a beam of 40 feet. She measured 1,994 gross tons and had the traditional East Coast silhouette of American steamers of that period. The artwork added to the Postcard was done incorrectly, suggesting that her upper deck house closely bracketed the single tall smokestack. A close examination of the illustration indicates no upper deck house where the passengers are standing on the upper deck just aft of the stack. It began shortly before the main mast, but the artist left the space white under what may be a cargo boom that seems to link the base of the stack with the start of the upper aft deck house.

The *ST. CROIX* operated from Boston, MA to Portland, Lubec and Eastport, ME, and then on to St. John, Newfoundland and New Brunswick, Nova Scotia. The steamer was sold to the Enterprise Transportation Company on November 7, 1906. Three years later, the ship was taken to the West Coast for passenger and cargo service to Nome, AK. The *ST. CROIX* burned near Santa Monica, CA, on November 11, 1911, with 169 persons aboard. Fortunately, all of the people aboard were saved, but the ship was a total loss.

The *ST. LOUIS* was built for the American Line, a part of the J.P. Morgan consortium called the International Mercantile Marine. The ship was the first top class liner built in the United States for service on the North Atlantic after the Civil War. She was christened in Philadelphia, PA, by Mrs. Grover Cleveland, wife of the President. The President stood beside her with 25,000 flag-waving Americans on November 12, 1884. The new ship was built by William Cramp, who stated proudly that "No Foreign Materials" went into the construction.

The vessel measured approximately 12,000 gross tons, a length of 554 feet, with a beam of 63 feet. The twin-screw ship had quadruple expansion engines of 20,500 horsepower with a speed of 21 knots. The *ST. LOUIS* began service in June 1885 with a passenger list of 320 persons in First Class. Among the First Class features were 6-foot, 6-inch beds, and the 1,200 electric light bulbs throughout the vessel. Her watertight bulkheads had no doors or openings up to the main deck for greater built-in safety. In World War I the ship was renamed *LOUISVILLE*. She burned while being refitted and was scuttled. In 1924 the old ship was towed to Italy and scrapped. The ship had a length of 277 feet, a width of 38 feet, and measured 1,676 gross tons. The boiler steam pressure was 160 pounds-per-square-inch, considerably higher than in earlier steamers. Note that the twin stacks are placed side by side. The ship made the overnight run from Bangor, ME to Boston, MA.

The Maine Steamship Company's ship *HORATIO HALL* was built in 1898 by the Delaware Iron Works, Chester, PA, The vessel was an identical sister craft to the *JOHN ENGLIS*. A third sister was named *NORTH STAR*. The *HORATIO HALL* spent her entire brief life of 12 years on run between Portland, ME and New York City. The ship measured 3,168 gross tons, a length of 297 feet, and a beam of 46 feet. She was fast, being able to make 16 knots with triple expansion engines. Only 22 hours were required to travel the 390 miles. Unfortunately, the ship had a sad ending. While off the shoals of Nantucket, MA, on March 10, 1909, the ship col-

S. S. Horatio Hall—Maine S. S. Co.

Publisher: G.W.Morris, Portland, ME • Manufacturer: Made In Germany • Type: Colored Dull Finish Photograph • Postmark: New London, CT, July 27, 1908 • Value Index: D

lided with a freighter, the *HENRY F. DIMOCK*, owned by the Metropolitan Line. Fortunately, the freighter was held in the big hole in the liner's side to prevent the *HORATIO HALL* from going down immediately. All the passengers and crew of the stricken vessel were taken on the freighter, an heroic feat in itself, in light of the fact that the *HENRY F.DIMOCK* was also badly damaged and had to be beached to avoid sinking. The following day the HORATIO HALL rolled over into deep water and was a complete loss.

Constructed in 1898 at Wilmington, DE for the Hartford & New York Transportation Company, the 1,240 gross ton *TENNESSEE* is shown under Joy Line management. The ship measured 245 feet in length, a beam of 38 feet, and a depth of 15.8 feet. The crew numbered 47 people and the engines had 2,100 horsepower. The vessel was built along traditional overnight steamer lines of the time period. With a narrow hull and twin screws, the ship could make 18 knots and was known as an excellent boat.

The Joy Line bought the vessel in 1906 and used the steamer on their

Joy Line Steamer Tennessee.

Publisher: R.Wilkinson, 55 Eddy Street, Providence, RI, Card No. VHC346 • Manufacturer: Not Indicated • Type: Colored Dull Finish Photograph • Postmark: Not Used • Value Index: E

run between Fall River, RI and New York City. In 1907, the *TENNESSEE* collided with the three-masted schooner *MIRONUS*, sinking the latter with the loss of four of the six-man crew. From 1910 to 1931 the steamer ran on the Bay State Line between New York City and Providence, RI. In 1936 the vessel, renamed *ROMANCE* by a new owner, was hit and sunk by the Sound steamer NEW YORK, owned by the Eastern SS Company.

The *CHESTER W. CHAPIN*, whose life span was to cover half a century, was built in 1899 at Sparrows Point, MD for the New England Steamship Company. The ship was used on their overnight service from New London, CT to New York City. The steamer measured 2,868 gross tons, a length of 312 feet, and a beam of 64 feet. The most distinctive part of the CHAPIN's exterior design was the vessel's twin stacks, decidedly close together. Mr.A. Carey Smith designed this fine craft. The ship's 4,200 horsepower provided a top speed of 18 knots to permit the voyage to New York City without racing.

Publisher: J. Solomon, New London, CT • Manufacturer: Made In USA...M • Type: Colored Dull Finish Photgraph • Postmark: Not Used • Value Index: D

A crew of 82 was evidence of a high standard of service. The high stern flag pole suggests this view was taken early in the ship's career, probably before World War I. Shortly before World War II the *CHESTER W. CHAPIN* was sold to the Colonial Line and renamed *METEOR*. A substantial rebuilding left the ship with one thick stack and improved the vessel's appearance. The ship became known as the ``Yankee Flagship'' and was operated between New York City and New Bedford, MA. Then the *METEOR* was acquired by the Old Bay Line and later by the Norfolk & Washington Line to be operated for more years as an overnight boat on Chesapeake Bay. The *METEOR* was scrapped without fanfare in 1948. Note, in the illustration, that the bow portion of the *HORATIO HALL* is raised to match the height of the first passenger promenade deck, and that the pilot house is on top of the two-deck superstructure. The helmsman had a place high enough to see over the bow, an important evolutionary step in American liner design.

The *GOVERNOR DINGLEY* began life with the spotlight of national publicity as this steamer was a replacement for the ill-fated *PORTLAND*. The *PORTLAND* was lost with all hands when she sank in a hurricane on the night of November 26, 1898, en route from Portland, ME to Boston, MA. The *GOVERNOR DINGLEY* was constructed by the Delaware River Iron & Shipbuilding Company of Chester, PA and launched on Sept. 5, 1899. The owners, Eastern Steamship Company, designed the craft with new lines. The hull was steel and the paddle wheels were replaced by propellers. The ship had 3,826 gross

Str. Governor Dingley.

Publisher: G.W. Morris, Portland, ME • Manufacturer: Made In Germany • Type: Colored Artist Conception • Postmark: Camden, ME, September 13, 1910 • Value Index: D

tonnage, a length of 298 feet, and a beam of 60 feet. The steamer was to make the overnight run to Boston, MA with a speed of 16 knots.

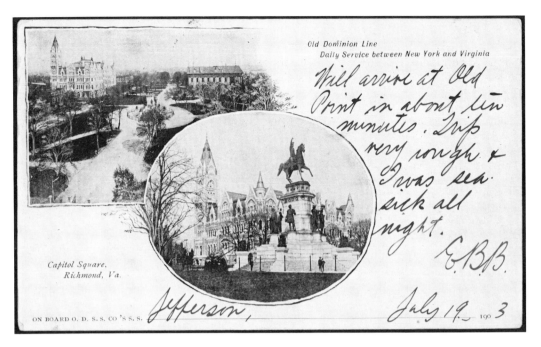

Old Dominion Line
Daily Service between New York and Virginia

Will arrive at Old
Point in about ten
minutes. Trip
very rough &
I was sea
sick all
night.
E.B.B.

Capitol Square,
Richmond, Va.

ON BOARD O. D. S. S. CO 'S S. S. *Jefferson,* July 19, 190 3

Publisher: Old Dominion Line • Manufacturer: Not Indicated • Type: Black-White Dull Finish Photograph • Postmark: Fortress Monroe, July 19, 1903 • Value Index: D

Publisher: Valley Publishing Company, 955 Main Street, Bridgeport, CT • Manufacturer: Dextone-Dexter Press, Pearl River, NY • Type: Colored Glossy Photograph • Postmark: Not Used • Value Index: D

This illustration is not a picture of a steamer or an interior of a ship. However, the information with the photographs is important to our history. It was issued aboard the new steamer *JEFFERSON* of the Old Dominion Line in daily service between New York City and Norfolk, VA. At the lower left in small print is the line: "ON BOARD O.D.S.S. CO'S S.S. (with *JEFFERSON* written in by hand)." The date: July 19, 1903. The *JEFFERSON* and *HAMILTON* were sisterships. Both were constructed in 1899 for Old Dominion Line. Each ship had 3,723 gross tons, was 251 feet long, and 42 feet wide. The boilers had 190 pounds-per-square-inch steam pressure, a great advance over earlier steamers. Both were modern, fast passenger-cargo ships. They were cut down during World War I for use by the U.S. Government as cargo ships and then restored to their owners and rebuilt with passenger spaces restored. In the process of rebuilding each ship was cut in half and new midships sections inserted to make them 24 feet longer. The Old Dominion Line was formed in 1867, offering overnight service between New York City and Norfolk, VA. In time, the company was absorbed by the Eastern Steamship Line.

Built in 1899, the ferryboat *BRINCKERHOFF* ran from Poughkeepsie, NY to Highland-on-Hudson, NY until 1942. The 140-foot craft was a double ender; that is, it could go either way with twin pilot houses facing opposite directions. The steamer was fitted with a walking beam engine by the Fletcher Iron Works, famous New York City engine builders. After four decades of Hudson River ferry work the craft was acquired by Bridgeport, CT for the short run on Long Island Sound to Pleasure Island Beach, NY. After seven years of this service the *BRINCKERHOFF* was laid up at Roundout Creek, NY. The Steamship Historical Society of America led by F. R. Hathaway of Noank, CT and W. H. Ewen of Hastings-on-Hudson, NY saved the ferry for the Mystic Seaport museum's fleet of historic sailing ships. The Fletcher walking beam engine, made with the care and precision of a fine watch had to be saved. Mayor Jasper McLevy of Bridgeport came to New York City for the donation of the boat to the Society. Later, after being towed to the Society, the ship was sold and moved away for use as a restaurant. After months of neglect, the venerable craft was destroyed by fire.

This fine vessel was built in 1899 for the North German Lloyd Line. The ship was first named *GROSSER KURFURST*. Constructed by the F. Schichau yard in Danzig, the liner had 13,245 gross tonnage, a length of 580 feet, and a beam of 62 feet. With twin screws and a quadruple expansion engine the ship was able to make 16 knots. The North German Lloyd Line used the vessel on their premier run to New York City and in Australian service. When the United States entered World War I in 1917, the liner was seized in New York City and renamed *AEOLUS* for

Publisher: Munson Steamship Line • Manufacturer: Not Indicated • Type: Sepia Dull Finish Photograph • Postmark: Wilm...PA, Dec...1921 • Value Index: D

use as an American troopship. This photograph, taken after the war, shows the shields of the United States Shipping Board on the twin stacks. The photograph was published by the Munson Line. This company, to make the ship seem larger, gave the vessel's displacement tonnage of 21,000 gross tons. This form of tonnage is generally not given for passenger ships. In 1922 the Munson Line gave up the *AEOLUS* and the Shipping Board assigned her to the Los Angeles Steamship Company (Lassco Line). The vessel, renamed *CITY OF LOS ANGELES*, was refurbished for a new run linking Los Angeles, CA with Honolulu, HI beginning in September 1922. Laid up in 1937 the *CITY OF LOS ANGELES* was sold to Japan.

The *NANTUCKET* was built in 1899 for the Merchants & Miners Line, and operated on the run between Boston, MA and Norfolk and Newport News, VA. Note the passengers on the sharply rising foredeck. The Jack (many-starred merchant marine flag at the bow) is shown standing out from its tall flag pole. Coal is being loaded on the port side, and the bow lines are taut. The ship's large searchlight is covered to protect it from erosion by salt spray. This picture exhibits the fine "Ship Shape" tradition of American coastal shipping built up over one-half century following the Civil War. The author is happy to say that this tradition is not dead. At this writing new ferries and new overnight steamers are being built and put into service on many routes around America suggesting that our country is returning with enthusiasm to her traditional water routes.The *NANTUCKET* was built by Harlan & Hollingsworth Company, Wilmington, DE. With 4,315 gross tons, the ship was 298 feet long, and a beam of 42 feet. Two pole masts were modern looking, but they could be rigged for sails.

Publisher: Steamship Historical Society of America • Manufacturer: Not Indicated • Type: Black-White Glossy Photograph • Postmark: Not Used • Value Index: E

The large shipping empire built up before World War I by the shipping genius for all time, Albert Ballin, made his Hamburg American Line the greatest ship line in number of ships, size of ships, and world impact. Certainly the motto of the company "The world is our field" was a goal that had been achieved by 1914 and no other ship line has accomplished.

One of the many German liners seized in America during April 1917 was the *HAMBURG*. This steamer had been built in 1899 by the Vulkan works at Stettin, Germany. In a relatively short life the *HAMBURG* had six names. This 10,532 gross ton

Dampfer „New-Rochelle" in Bremerhaven ankommend

Publisher: Not Indicated • Manufacturer: Made In Germany • Type: Black-White Dull Finish Photograph • Postmark: Not Used • Value Index D

steamer initially sailed in Hapag's Far East service. In 1904 the 499-foot-long steamer was moved to the New York City run. When the ship's American career began it was discovered that the engines had been sabotaged by the German crew. Restored in record time, the steamer was renamed *RED CROSS* and used briefly as a hospital ship. Later she became the *NEW ROCHELLE* , as shown here.

The sisterships *PONCE* and *SAN JUAN* were built at Wilmington, DE in 1899. Launching was in September 1899 and they began service three months later for the New York City and Porto Rico Line (old spelling). The company had two principal passenger routes, the 1,380-mile run from Puerto Rico to New York City and the 1,565-mile service to New Orleans, LA. They also had freighter services to Port Arthur and Galveston, TX. The *PONCE*, shown in this illustration, had space for 83 passengers. Passenger space was spread over three decks

Publisher: Porto Rico Line • Manufacturer: Albertype Company, Brooklyn, NY • Type: Black-White Dull Finish Photograph • Postmark: Not Used • Value Index: E

on this 3,503 gross ton ship. In 1913 fares from New York City to San Juan, PR ranged from $65 to $80 in First Class. Second Class cabins could be had for $45 to $50. Wages were $140 a month for pursers, surgeons received $115 a month, and seamen were paid $20 a month. In 1913 the steamer was fitted with wireless. The public rooms would seem very small by today's standards. The fleet in 1924 included the old steamer *PORTO RICO*, the *SAN JUAN*, the *PONCE*, and the flagship *SAN LORENZO*. In the period between the World Wars the Porto Rico Line came under the control of the large holding company known as AGWI, the Atlantic, Gulf and West Indies Lines. The PONCE and the *SAN JUAN* were converted into cargo ships in 1938 and shortly after the conversion were laid up and scrapped.

The profession of naval architecture and marine engineering is known for anonymity. One of few to be known was Frank Kerby, of Great Lakes and Hudson River fame . His best-known ship was the excursion steamer *TASHMOO*. The *TASHMOO* was painted white, was long, sleek, and looked handsome from every angle. One short mast atop the pilot house, two properly designed smokestacks, and the steamer's name in large letters on the paddle box provided a special distinction to the *TASHMOO*. No walking beam was visible. The ship was 302 feet in length, and measured 1,344 gross tons. The TASHMOO was built in 1900 at Wyandotte, MI for

Steamer Tashmoo.

Publisher: Not Indicated, Card No. 2716 • Manufacturer: Not Indicated • Type: Colored Glossy Photograph • Postmark: Detroit, MI, September 10, 1912 • Value Index E

the White Star Navigation Company of Detroit, MI. A highpoint of the steamer's career was a race on June 4, 1901 with the *CITY OF ERIE*. The weather was perfect. The *CITY OF ERIE*'s Master stowed his lifeboats on the lower deck to reduce wind resistance and removed all flag poles. His Chief Engineer Rendall was ready and the firemen were sorting coal to make sure there were no pieces that looked stony and might cause clinkers under the huge boilers. Similar preparations were being made aboard the *TASHMOO*. Ohioans supported the *CITY OF ERIE*. The *TASHMOO* was Detroit's favorite.

The race started six miles outside of the Cleveland, OH breakwater and finished at the Presque Isle Lighthouse, Erie, PA. The *CITY OF ERIE* won by 45 seconds. Despite the loss the TASHMOO became the best known steamer on the Great Lakes running until 1936. In 1988 the TASHMOO was elected to the National Maritime Hall of Fame at the American Merchant Marine Museum.

Captain Charles E. Pearsall owned several steamers, including the little one shown here. He used them as excursion boats operating out of Yonkers, NY. He and the author were active in the Steamship Historical Society during the World War II period. This Postcard was given to the author as a gift in 1942. The *COMET* was built in 1901 at Portland, ME. With an overall length of only 85 feet and a 22-foot beam, the ship measured 77 gross tons. The *COMET* had a 250-passenger capacity. Captain Pearsall bought this craft in 1918 at the end of World War I. At first he operated the vessel as a Yonkers, NY to Alpine ferry; later he expanded the excursion boat field by operating out of New York City up Long Island Sound, and from the Hudson River to New Brunswick, NJ.

Excursion Steamer "Comet,"
C. E. & E. H. Pearsall,
Yonkers, N. Y.
Telephone Yonkers 3937.

Publisher: C.E. & E.H. Pearsall, Yonkers, NY • Manufacturer: E.C.Kroff, Milwaukee, WI • Type: Black-White Dull Finish Photograph • Postmark: Not Used • Value Index D

The steel-hulled, single screw liner *APACHE* was built in 1901 for the Clyde Line, a company whose ships were named after Indian tribes. The new craft was 336 feet in length, had a beam of 46 feet, and measured 4,145 gross tons. These dimensions made the ship one of the largest coastal steamers under the American flag. There was space for steerage passengers, generally servants, in the forecastle of the hurricane deck.

A 1914 brochure indicated the Clyde Line fleet as numbering 22 steamers, aggregating 56,826 tons. On November 5, 1921, when

Publisher: Clyde Steamship Company • Manufacturer: Not Indicated • Black-White Artist Conception • Postmark: Wall Street Station, NY • Value Index D

10 miles north of Fenwick Island Light off the Delaware coast, the *APACHE* hit a five-masted schooner named the *SINGLETON PALMER*. The sailing ship sank, with the loss of one member of the 12-man crew. The *APACHE* suffered only a hole under the starboard anchor, which was repaired quickly at the Tietjen & Land yard in New York City. Her regular route linked Boston, MA, New York City, Baltimore, MD, Charleston, SC, Brunswick, Canada, and Jacksonville, and Sanford, FL. Late in 1924 Miami, FL was included as a new stop on the itinerary. The *APACHE* had a reputation as a fine ship and lived a good life.

The *NEW SHORE-HAM* shown in this illustration was a ferry. There was a cargo port for automobiles, although when the vessel was new in 1901 this entrance was probably used to bring produce aboard in horse-drawn wagons. Also a small dining saloon decorated with all the steamboat elegance the town of New Shoreham, RI could afford. The ferry is reputed to actually have bankrupted the town. The steamer was built by William McKie, of Boston, MA, and ran between Providence and Block Island, RI from 1901 through 1929. The town of New Shoreham was located on

Publisher: Ye Postte Cardde Shoppe, Block Island, RI • Manufacturer: Not Indicated • Type: Colored Dull Finish Photograph • Postmark: Not Used • Value Index: D

the Island. The *NEW SHOREHAM* measured 503 gross tons, had a length of 152 feet, and a beam of 28 feet. The two tall pole masts do not seem to be rigged with sail. Note the old fashioned anchor resting on the foredeck. Marine design changed very slowly. In later years the *NEW SHOREHAM* was renamed twice, becoming the *MYRTLE* II and then the *PRICILLA ALDEN*. The steamer served as an excursion boat in Boston Harbor, and then between Boston and Plymouth, MA. The sturdy vessel ran as a ferry from Bridgeport, CT to Port Jefferson, NY and was scrapped in 1955 at the age of 55.

"MONGOLIA" "MANCHURIA"
"CHINA"
SPEED   "KOREA" "SIBERIA"   COMFORT

TONNAGE
27,000.
SPEED
18 KNOTS.
TWIN SCREWS.

SAN FRANCISCO,
HONOLULU,
YOKOHAMA,
KOBE,
NAGASAKI,
SHANGHAI,
HONG KONG,
MANILA.

TRANS-PACIFIC LINE, PACIFIC MAIL STEAMSHIP CO.

Publisher: National Maritime Mueseum, San Francisco, CA • Manufacturer: Not Indicated • Type: Black-White Artist Conception • Postmark: Not Used • Value Index: F

Publisher:Smith Gallery, 1045 Madison Avenue, New York, NY • Manufacturer: Not indicated • Type: Colored Artist Conception • Postmark: Not Used • Value Index: F

From the Civil War until World War II the bulk of America's maritime enterprise was in coastal, Great Lakes, and river steamers. In 1901 two 11,785 gross ton liners, *KOREA* and *SIBERIA*, were built for the Pacific Mail Line. By custom it used foreign seamen under American officers. They were built by Newport News SB & DD Company and were the first big passenger ships constructed in America since the *ST. LOUIS* and the *ST. PAUL* of 1895. Each ship was 572 feet long and had a beam of 63 feet. They were twin screw steamers with a speed of 17 knots. The two ships operated to the Orient linking San Francisco, CA with Honolulu, HI, Japan, China, and the Philippines. A round trip required two months. One unusual feature was the promenade-like passage on the port side of the upper deck on the *KOREA* and the *SIBERIA*. On the starboard side this area was plain hull plating and portholes; a completely different appearance depending on which side you looked at the ship.

A brochure proudly listed the "American Features" offered: "Wireless telegraphy, submarine signal service, bilge keels, double bottoms, water-tight bulkheads, electric fan in each stateroom, electric reading light in each berth, electric fans in Dining Room, and swimming tank on deck, Filipino band of stringed instruments, concerts each afternoon and evening, games and amusements." Something that was not mentioned was a small room in the crew area for opium smoking. The *KOREA* and the *SIBERIA* were sold to Toyo Kisen Kaisha, a Japanese line. Each was renamed becoming the *KOREA MARU* and the *SIBERIA MARU*. Both were broken up in Japan in 1935.

At least three major passenger ships have been named *MORRO CASTLE*. The earliest, a paddle steamer, was burned in 1883. This illustration shows the *MORRO CASTLE* (No. 2) of 1901, a steel-hulled beauty ordered by the Ward Line for its service between New York City and Havana, Cuba. Built by William Cramp of Philadelphia, PA, this vessel was a large ship, measuring 6,004 gross tons. The ship was 400 feet long and had a beam of 50 feet. This *MORRO CASTLE* had a successful life until the owners became involved in complicated merger and financial dealing in the early 1920s. She was sold at auction for a mere $28,000 on July 31, 1924 and presumably scrapped in 1925.

This illustration is a painting of the *MORRO CASTLE* of 1901 by the famous Danish-American marine artist Antonio Nicolo Gasparo Jacobsen. Note the large square windows on the *MORRO CASTLE*'s main deck below the white-painted superstructure. Such windows were an innovation in 1901. Today's cruise ships use similarly shaped windows and call them innovative. No sails are shown in the picture, although it is likely that the *MORRO CASTLE* had them.

The company had evolved into one of the largest of American coastal steamship lines. It was struck down in 1934 and 1935 with three disasters, the grounding of their *HAVANA*, the burning of the *MORRO CASTLE* (of 1930), and the sinking of the *MOHAWK* (owned by an Agwi Lines subsidiary and chartered to the Ward Line).

The ship in this illustration is the *NORTH STAR*, of the Maine SS Company one of the companies which merged to form Eastern Steamship Lines. The vessel has the outline known as the "Maine Coastal Line Design" including a tall stack, superstructure all the way to the stern, a built up forecastle enveloping the forward part of the main deck, and a string of lifeboats on the boat deck. Two sturdy masts, looking short in contrast to the decidedly tall black smokestack, and the traditional tall flag poles at bow and stern complete the silhouette. The *NORTH STAR* was built in 1901 and there were two

Publisher: G.W. Morris, Portland, ME • Manufacturer: Made In Germany • Type: Colored Dull Finish Photograph • Postmark: Brooklyn, NY, July 18, 1904 • Value Index: D

sistersships, the *HORATION HALL* and the *JOHN ENGLIS*. The Postcard was written aboard the steamer which had just docked at Philadelphia, PA. Perhaps the sender gave it to the purser at the landing who took it back to Maine the next night and mailed it. The *NORTH STAR* was built at Chester, PA and measured 3,159 gross tons, had a length of 299 feet, and a beam of 46 feet. The ship was able to reach a speed of 16 knots between Portland, ME and New York City. The steamer occasionally ran between Boston, MA and Yarmouth, Nova Scotia. The *NORTH STAR* had an abrupt ending on August 8, 1919, with 348 passengers aboard when the sturdy vessel ran on Green Island Ledge. All people were saved, but the ship was a total loss.

This illustration shows the American deep-sea liner, *FINLAND*. This ship had an important life. When initially operated by the Red Star Line, the ship was painted by one of the finest Postcard artists, H. Cassiers. The *FINLAND* is painted in gray-blue on white. It shows the handsome two-stacked steamship steaming away and a small boat in the foreground. Four liners of this class built with the *FINLAND* and *KROONLAND* as the American pair. Their two sisters (*VADERLAND AND ZEELAND*) were foreign-built and flew the flags of Belgium or Great Britain. J.P. Morgan

Publisher: Red Star Line • Manufacturer: Not Indicated • Type: Painting by H. Cassiers (Blue-Gray) • Postmark: Not Used • Value Index: E

had ordered them for his International Mercantile Marine's Red Star Line, all of whose ships had names ending with the suffix "land." They served occasionally under the American Line house flag, as Morgan had the custom of freely shifting ships between his lines. They were large-sized ships for the time period, but not the largest type. Each measured 12,188 gross tons. The FINLAND had a length of 580 feet, two feet longer than the sistership and 60 feet in width. They had twin screws, each producing 9,200 horsepower with boilers of 170 pounds-per-square-inch steam pressure and could reach a speed of 16 knots. The two liners were scrapped in 1927.

ON BOARD OLD DOMINION LINE STEAMSHIP "BERKELEY"...................191

Publisher: Old Dominion Line • Manufacturer: Not Indicated, Card No. 58-771 • Type: Colored Glossy Photograph • Postmark: Not Used • Value Index: D

Two quite different pre-World War I Postcards for two almost identical companion ships are illustrated. Both Postcards have the same printing at top and bottom, except for the name of the ship. The two illustrations are quite different. At the bottom of the Postcards the space was provided for the passenger to insert the date, any year between 1910 and 1919. The twin ships were built in 1902. The *BERKLEY* Postcard shows a black stack with a yellow band. This coloring was a printer's error, as the Old Dominion Line had a red band on its tall black stacks. There appears to be a faint red tinge to the stack band on the *BRANDON* Postcard. The *BRANDON* was built at Wilmington, DE. The author has not been able to confirm that the sistership was constructed at the same place; however, this use of one location would seem likely. The *BERKLEY* was a trifle larger, with 1,075 gross tons in comparison to the *BRANDON*'s 1,062 tons. Both had 170 pounds-per-square-inch steam pressure in their boilers, indicating that their engineering design was state of the art. The two steamers each measured 200 feet in length and 39 feet wide.

ON BOARD OLD DOMINION LINE STEAMSHIP "BRANDON"...................191

Publisher: Old Dominion Line • Manufacturer: Not Indicated, Card No. 58-770 • Type: Colored Glossy Photograph • Postmark: Not Used • Value Index: D

6078 STR. " WESTERN STATES, " DETROIT AND BUFFALO.

Publisher: Detroit Photgraphic Company, Card No. 6078 • Manufacturer: Not Indicated • Type: Colored Dull Finish Photograph • Postmark: Not Used • Value Index: E

Two sisterships illustrated here were successful and long-lived Great Lakes overnight boats, the *WESTERN STATES* and *EASTERN STATES*. They were built at Wyandotte, MI in 1902. Each was in turn a flagship of the Detroit & Cleveland Navigation Company of Detroit, MI.

The illustration of the *WESTERN STATES* shows a full starboard broadside with eight flags and pennants flying, a large Bone In Her Teeth (wave mass right at the stem where the bow cuts through the water), and white foam where the paddle wheel is churning up the Lake. A tail of black coal smoke puffs out of the single stack.

The illustration of the *EASTERN STATES* shows the ship steaming away from Buffalo, NY. The two ships had identical dimensions, 350 feet long and 44 feet wide. Both measured 3,077 gross tons, had 4,200 horsepower with six boilers designed for 140 pounds-per-square-inch of steam pressure. A study of their deck plans indicates only two passenger decks. No public rooms are shown, although the long area between the two rows of staterooms was known as the "Gallery" and did have couches and easy chairs. A dining saloon was on the lower deck aft. Somewhere there would have been a small smoking room. These steamers were not as luxurious as their successors would be.

Steamer "Eastern States," Buffalo, N. Y.

Publisher: Not Indicated, Card No. A-6204 • Manufacturer: Not Indicated • Type: Colored Glossy Photograph • Postmark: Not Used • Value Index: E

The *MERION*, of the American line, was a foreign flag vessel owned by J.P. Morgan in his International Mercantile Marine. The steamship was built in 1902 by the John Brown Shipyard on the Clyde, England, builders of many great ships, including the *QUEEN MARY*. The *MERION* measured 11,612 gross tons, was 547 feet in length, and had a beam of 59 feet. The silhouette was typical of the time period with four masts and one smokestack. Triple expansion engines offered a speed of only 12 knots. Speed was not critical as the ship was designed to carry 150 passengers in Second Class and 1,700

Publisher: American Line, Card No. 202920 • Manufacturer: State Publishing Company, Liverpool, NY • Type: Colored Glossy Photograph • Postmark: Not Used • Value Index: D

passengers in Third Class. A sistership called the *HAVERFORD* was built one year earlier. As was the custom with Morgan, the *MERION* was shifted from one service to another. The first crossing made by the new vessel was from Liverpool, England to Boston, MA under the Dominion Line house flag on March 8, 1902. Within a short time the new ship was transferred to the American Line and operated from Liverpool, England to Philadelphia, PA. During World War I, the steamer was converted by the British Navy into a dummy battleship. On May 30, 1915 the vessel was sunk in the Aegean Sea by a German torpedo. This illustration of the *MERION* shows the ship in the colors of the American Line, with crossed British and United States flags.

This coastal ferry is the Vineyard Ferryboat *UNCATENA*, which proudly carried an old Indian name of the area. The steamer was built by the Pusey & Jones Company at Wilmington, DE in 1902, measured 652 gross tons and a length of 178 feet. Functional in design, the ferry had no masts, but two tall flag poles at bow and stern. The single smokestack was very tall and supported by at least four guy wires. Between 1902 and 1929 the *UNCATENA* was used to link New Bedford, CT. with the Nantucket SB Company. This illustration does not show much of the steamer, however, the

STR. UNCATENA, OAK BLUFFS, MASS.

Publisher: J.N. Chamberlain, Oak Bluffs, MA, Card No. 76918 • Manufacturer: C.T. American Art • Type: Colored Dull Finish Photograph • Postmark: Not Used • Value Index: E

excitement of the bow view has more feeling to it. Also appealing is the cutting of the water at the stem, the spreading pattern of waves from the paddle wheels, and the wake that shows the *UNCATENA* has just made a sharp turn to starboard. All of these factors plus the delightful group of women in their old-style dresses provide a fascinating picture. There was a fire in 1929 and it ended *UNCATENA*'s career. She was sold to the Nantucket SB Company and served them until being scrapped at Quincy, MA in 1937.

STEAMER "ASBURY PARK,"
FLAGSHIP NEW JERSEY CENTRAL'S
SANDY HOOK ROUTE

The *ASBURY PARK* sailed from New York City to the Atlantic Highlands. The steamer was the flagship of the New Jersey Central's Sandy Hook Line and became one of the longest-lived and most successful of all American coastal ships. The ship measured 3,016 gross tons. With 5,900 horsepower this vessel may have been the fastest ship in the American Merchant Marine when she was built in Philadelphia, PA in 1903. The steamer was used with the *MONMOUTH* and *SANDY HOOK*. Their assignment was to get wealthy commuters to and from New York's Manhattan as

Publisher: Union News Company, New York, NY, Card No. 1163 • Manufacturer: Not Indicated • Type: Colored Glossy Photograph • Postmark: Newburgh, NY, September 10, 1912 • Value Index: D

quickly as possible. The *ASBURY PARK*'s tremendous air funnels attest to her great power. The ship's dimensions were 297 feet long and 50 feet wide.

The second career of this vessel began in 1917, when the Monticello SS Company of San Francisco bought the steamer. The veteran was sold, put on another run, and renamed *CITY OF SACRAMENTO*. While the new *DELTA KING* and *DELTA QUEEN* did the nightly boat service on the river route to Sacramento, CA, the *CITY OF SACRAMENTO* performed the daytime trip. In 1944 the Black Ball Line bought the old vessel for ferry service in British Columbia, Canada. The ship was rebuilt and renamed *KAHLOKE*, meaning White Swan in the language of the local Indians. Capacity was 100 cars or trucks with 1,000 passengers. Four 1,750 horsepower engines provided a speed of 20 knots. The old steamer was sold again and renamed *LANGDALE QUEEN*. Lastly, the craft was sold, became the *LADY GRACE,* and converted to use as a pontoon in Howe Sound.

STEAMER EASTERN S. S. LINES, EASTPORT—ST. JOHN—BOSTON.

The *CALVIN AUSTIN* was large, beautiful, and commodious. From the new-style Patent anchor to the four-deck tier at the stern this steamer was a 20th-century design. The Eastern Steamship Lines built this ship in 1903 to run from Eastport, ME to St. John, New Brunswick, to Boston, MA. The *AUSTIN* was launched in 1903 at the Delaware River Iron & SB Company yard, Chester, PA. The ship's perfectly straight stem, two sharply raked pole masts, and tall single smokestack was an outstanding design of the time period. During World War I this

Publisher: Eastern SS Lines, Card No. 122958 • Manufacturer: Tichnor Quality Views • Colored Dull Finish Photograph • Postmark: Not Used • Value Index: E

vessel served the country as a United States Shipping Board training ship. Between 1918 and 1934 the *AUSTIN* was used on the Boston to New York Line and between Portland, ME and Boston. On July 3, 1934, the *CALVIN AUSTIN* was sold for scrapping.

A Mr. Twaddle used this Postcard to write to a lad named Abbot Wilson of New Rochelle, NY on August 25, 1912, four months after the sinking of the *TITANIC*, never dreaming that the *EASTLAND* would be thought of as an American *TITANIC* within less than three years. The *EASTLAND* was built in 1903 for the Eastland Navigation Company with a length of 269 feet and a width of 36 feet. Rumors describing the lack of stability for this ship were common from the beginning of the ship's use. In 1910 the owners ran an advertisement insisting that the ship was safe, noting that over 400,000 people had sailed aboard the *EASTLAND* in the four previous years.

Publisher: Cleveland News Company, Cleveland, OH, Card No. 4085 • Manufacturer: Not Indicated • Type: Colored Glossy Photograph • Postmark: Wakem, Ohio, August 26, 1912 • Value Index: D

On July 24, 1915, the ship was at a pier in Chicago preparing to leave on an excursion to Michigan City. Aboard were employees of the Western Electric Company and a group from a local church for a total of 2,500 passengers. For some reason a number of them rushed to the port, or outboard side. Hundreds followed and the ship began to list jamming more people into the mass of bodies on the lower port side. The *EASTLAND* went over on its side and down in a depth of 21 feet of water. An estimated 835 died when trapped in their cabins or in the water when the steamer capsized. The hulk was raised and served for years as a government survey ship.

The *TIONESTA* was one of three ships built for the long run between Buffalo, NY and Duluth, MI between 1902 and 1910. They were owned by the Erie & Western Transit Company popularly known as the Anchor Line, and by the Pennsylvania Railroad Company. The ships were built at Wyandotte, MI by the Detroit SB Company and brought a new level of luxury to service on overnight steamers for the Great Lakes.

This illustration is a photograph taken in the early days of the *TIONESTA* before a second or upper promenade deck was added to increase the passenger capacity. The *TIONESTA* had a crew of 144 people. These ships

Publisher: Anchor Line (Photograph by Wickman) Card No. 1552G • Manufacturer: Made In Germany • Sepia Tone Dull Finish Photograph • Postmark: Not Used • Value Index: E

pioneered in a number of important new design features. Their engines were aft, unique at the turn of the century for passenger vessels. This design is now virtually standard for all new ships built throughout the world. Steam pressure in the boiler on the *TIONESTA* was 210 pounds-per-square inch, more than other ships of that period and produced 2,450 horsepower. The ship measured 4,333 gross tons, was 340 feet long, with a width of 45 feet.

This great ship, the *KAISER WILHELM II* (1903), deserves a place in this history. For 14 years the vessel was the pride of the North German Lloyd Line, winning the Blue Ribbon of the Atlantic Ocean. Then, for 23 years the ship was under the flag of the United States. In World War I the four-stacker served as the American transport *AGAMEMNON*, then for the remaining years was renamed *MONTICELLO* and laid up in James River, VA. During this long period of idleness almost continuous efforts were made to return the steamship to active service. The tragedy is that

Publisher: North German Lloyd, Bremen, Germany • Manufacturer: The PCK Series • Type: Color Glossy Painting • Postmark: Not Used • Value Index: E

after being kept in reserve for two decades the great ship was sold for scrap in 1940 to 1941, a few months before America's entry in World War II. No doubt the war would have seen the vessel required for troopship work.

Only 14 four-stacked passenger steamships were ever built for transocean service. They were outstanding examples of extravagant interior design, currently admired. Each ship had three-deck high-domed dining saloons, miles of carving and elegant joinerwork (wooden work on ships is known as joinerwork), mirrors, tapestries, grand staircases, and red carpets.

This ship stands out in the story of interesting ships. The *MONROE* had 4,500 horsepower, 4,704 gross tons, a length of 346 feet, and a beam of 46 feet. On November 3, 1906, the steamer was in a narrow channel near the Crany Island Lighthouse, between Hampton Roads and Norfolk, VA. Ahead of the ship was the new battleship *VIRGINIA*. The Old Dominion liner attempted to pass the battleship on the latter's starboard. At that time few people understood the suction power that came with massive hulls in narrow waterways.The *MONROE*'s Master had never experienced indraft. When he began to lose control of his

Publisher: Not Indicated, Card No. 63942 • Manufacturer: Not Indicated • Type: Colored Glossy Photograph • Postmark: Norfolk, VA, June 19, 1911 • Value Index: F

ship he tried to slow down. The ship's bow struck the *VIRGINIA*'s starboard quarter. Lifeboats were demolished on the warship and hull frames bent. A 3-inch gun was demolished. There were no casualties.

Captain Seaton Schroeder on the *VIRGINIA* had made every effort to avoid the *MONROE*. He ordered full speed while at hard right rudder and pointing across the narrow channel toward a lighthouse. The two lighthouse keepers were horrified at the sight of the warship speeding at them. They rushed to their small boat and rowed away as fast as they were able to move. Six-and-a-half years later the *MONROE*, near Hog Island, NY, was struck by the *NANTUCKET*, and went down in 30 minutes with the death of 23 passengers and 24 crew members.

San Jacinto

MALLORY STEAMSHIP COMPANY · SAN JACINTO
The Direct Passenger and Fast Freight "Ocean Route" from and to Texas and the Southwest
Galveston, Tex.   Mobile, Ala.   Tampa, Fla.   Key West, Fla.   New York

Publisher: Mallory Steamship Company • Manufacturer: Not Indicated • Type: Black-White Dull Finish Photograph • Postmark: Not Used • Value Index: E

Second to the Ward Line, the Mallory Line had one of the finest fleets of good-sized, ocean-going steamers in the American coastal trade. Their service was listed by the U.S. Government as noncontiguous, meaning that major segments of the run were out of sight of land. Linking Texas to New York City the Mallory Line steamers usually made stops at Galveston, TX, Mobile, AL, Tampa and Key West, FL. The Mallory Steamship Company advertisements called this the "Ocean Route." One of their ships was the dignified *SAN JAC-INTO*, built in 1903 by the Delaware River SB Company at Chester, PA. This ship measured 6,069 gross tons, with triple expansion engines and twin screws and a 15-knot-plus speed. As initially built the single smokestack was much taller than shown in this illustration. When forced draft was developed, the stack was reduced in size. The ship was 380 feet long and had a beam of 53 feet.

The *SAN JACINTO* was a good looking ship, although the silhouette was imperfect because the masts were not evenly spaced. In the latter part of the ship's career the steamer was bought by the Porto Rico Line (spelling correct for that day). The name was not changed. The *SAN JACINTO* was torpedoed and sunk on April 22, 1942.

Publisher: Not Indicated • Manufacturer: Not Indicated • Type: Poor Quality Glossy Photograph • Postmark: Not Used • Value Index: E

There is a true and somewhat poignant story about the *DAKOTA*, launched in 1904. It was one of two great ships built for the railroad tycoon James J. Hill on his trans-Pacific service. When the *DAKOTA* was ready for launching Hill, an old swashbuckler, planned to have the sponsor christen the ship with a bottle of wine. However, he became enmeshed in the battle for a constitutional amendment preventing the use of wine. A group of women from the North and South Dakota Territories asked him not to use the intoxicating beverage. He said no. The affronted women passed a resolution stating they hoped the ship would never make any money and would not have good fortune. Thousands of women signed it. The launching passed without incident as did the maiden trans-Pacific crossing in 1905. Then on March 3, 1907, the new ship ran aground near Japan and was a total loss.

The *DAKOTA* was rated at 20,714 gross tons, had a length of 622 feet, and a beam of 73 feet. The ship could make 17 knots, but the service speed was only 14 knots. In 1923 this ship was towed to Germany and scrapped.

"Gambling Prohibited" was the sign most evident in the small social hall aboard the *JEFFERSON*, of the Alaskan Steamship Company. The ship was built in 1904. The gambling sign was printed in large letters and it was fastened on the lower part of the foremast which rose through the center of the ship forward of the grand staircase. The ship catered to gold rush passengers and gambling was a favorite pastime for 21 years on the Alaskan run. The craft measured 1,615 gross tons, was 207 feet long, and 40 feet wide. The *JEFFERSON* was built at the Heath shipyard, Tacoma, WA. Triple expansion engines of 1,600 horsepower per-

Lowman & Hanford Company, Seattle, WA • Manufacturer: Photograph by F.H. Nowell • Type: Colored Glossy Photograph • Postmark: Not Used • Value Index: E

mitted a speed of 13 knots, a slow top speed. The crew numbered 60 persons. Captain Gus Nord, the ship's best known Master, had one of the longest careers as a skipper in Alaskan maritime history. Only one serious accident marred the liner's career. On November 23, 1904, the ship ran aground at Sheep Creek in the Gastineau Channel with a broken propeller.

Here is another American ship which began life and is remembered as a North German Lloyd (NGL) liner flying the German flag. As the *PRINZ EITEL FRIEDRICH*, the vessel was run for 13 years between ports in Europe and the Far East, via the Suez Canal. She was built in 1904 at the Vulcan Shipyard in Stettin, Germany. With a length of 506 feet, a beam of 55 feet, the vessel measured 8,797 gross tons. Twin screws and quadruple expansion engines gave the liner a speed of 16 knots. As initially designed, the steamship could take only 166 persons in First Class, 158 persons in Second Class, and 614 persons in Third

Publisher: North German Lloyd, Bremen, Germany • Manufacturer: Made In Germany • Type: Sepia Tone Glossy Photograph • Postmark: Not Used • Value Index: E

Class. During the early days of World War I, the *PRINZ EITEL* was run as a commerce raider. Taken over in 1917 by the United States the ship was renamed DE KALB to ferry U.S. troops to Europe.

In 1921 the liner was rebuilt as a passenger ship, with space for 100 persons in First Class and 1,000 persons in Third Class. The Shipping Board renamed the old ship *MOUNT CLAY*. The vessel ran under the United American Line house flag, serving between New York City and Hamburg, Germany. In 1934 the out-of-date craft was sold for scrap.

STEAMER JUNIATA, DULUTH-SUPERIOR HARBOR   118624

Publisher: R.D. Handy, Incorporated, Duluth, MN, Card No. 118624 • Manufacturer: C.T. American Art Colored • Type: Colored Dull Finish Photograph • Postmark: Not Used • Value Index: F

The *JUNIATA*, at this writing, is 90 years old and may sail again. The steamer is tied up to a pier in Chicago, IL awaiting modernization for a new passenger service. The ship's streamlined configiration does not suggest the fact that she was built in 1904 for the Anchor Line. With a measurement of 4,330 gross tons, the steamer is 361 feet long, 45 feet wide, and can carry 1,000 passengers with a crew of 150 people.

The upper promenade was described as being 376 feet long which is 15 feet longer than the measured length of the ship. This added length was accomplished by including the ship's wide beam at bow and stern as part of the walking distance, a bit of exaggeration. The engines were placed aft, anticipating the Matson Line pre-World War I design by a decade and far ahead of today's cruise ships.

The *JUNIATA* was modernized in 1941 and renamed *MILWAUKEE CLIPPER*. The ship could carry 900 passengers and 120 automobiles on the route between Milwaukee, WI and Muskegon, MI. After seven years of operation on this service the *JUNIATA* was laid up. She was purchased by the Great Lakes Transit Company of Chicago, IL. The steamer ran as an excursion boat, completing four trips a day from Chicago.

Publisher: The L.L. Cook Company, Milwaukee, WI • Manufacturer: Not Indicated • Type: Colored Glossy Photograph • Postmark: Milwaukee, WI, July 28, 1954 • Value Index: F

43

Postcards were given to passengers as the top or decorative part of a menu by several steamship lines in the early 1900s. This illustration was the *MONGOLIA*'s breakfast menu for Monday, August 16, 1919. Fortunately, the passenger kept it intact. Imagine selecting "Devilled Turkey Bones" for breakfast. The MONGOLIA was built for Atlantic Transport Lines in 1904 by the New York SB Corporation, Camden, NJ. The name was to have been *MINNELORA*, but J.P. Morgan's ship combine (International Mercantile Marine) was always in a state of flux and the ship was sold, with a sistership, to the Pacific Mail Line. Both ships measured 13,635 gross tons, were 616 feet long, and 65 feet wide. Each ship had four masts, a single large smokestack, was powered with quadruple expansion engines driving twin screws, and could make 16 knots. The sistership, originally to have been named *MINNEKAHDA*, came out as the *MANCHURIA*. Both were sold back to the Atlantic Transport Line in 1915 and kept their Pacific Mail names, serving as troopships in World War I.

After the end of the war the pair of ships ran on the Atlantic for the American Line and were then assigned to another of Morgan's subsidiary lines, the Panama Pacific Line and ran with the *FINLAND* and the *KROONLAND* on its new intercoastal service. They were painted white. In 1929 the two ships were renamed when acquired by the Dollar Line for around-the-world service. The *MONGOLIA* became the *PRESIDENT FILLMORE*, and The *MANCHURIA* was renamed *PRESIDENT JOHNSON*.

S. S. "MONGOLIA"

Monday   August   16th, 1909
BREAKFAST

Oranges   Stewed Prunes

CEREALS

Oat Meal Mush   Farina

Fish

Grilled Fish   Smoked Salmon

Steak......Broiled, to Order

Devilled Turkey Bones

Hashed Beef with Walnuts

Grilled,......Ham......and Bacon

Eggs   &   Omelette to Order

Potatoes Saute and Mashed Potatoes

Rolls, & Cakes, Etc

Vienna Rolls   Graham Rolls

Sally Lunn   Soda Biscuits

Buckwheat Cakes...and...Syrup

Cocoa   Tea   Coffee

Meal Hours.......Breakfast 8 a. m. to 9 a. m.

Ernest, L, Hawyes,   Frank, J, Leonard,
Chief Steward   Second Steward

Publisher: Pacific Mail Line • Manufacturer: Not Indicated • Type: Colored Dull Finish Painting (With Menu) • Postmark: Not Used • Value Index: B

UNITED STATES LINES   S. S. AMERICA   U. S. GOVERNMENT SHIP

Publisher: United States Lines • Manufacturer: Not Indicated • Type: Colored Glossy Painting • Postmark: Not Used • Value Index: C

When new in 1905 the *AMERIKA* was the largest ship in the world. Built for Hamburg American Line, the vessel was intended to carry 1,765 persons in Steerage (that class produced the profit) with 420 persons in First, 254 persons in Second, and 223 persons in Third Class. The ship was seized in New York during World War I and renamed *AMERICA*. Between World Wars I and II she represented America with distinction as running mate of the *GEORGE WASHINGTON* and the *LEVIATHAN*. During World War II the historic liner was again a troopship, this time renamed *EDMOND B. ALEXANDER*. When scrapped in 1958 she was 53 years old. The *AMERIKA-AMERICA* was notable for several firsts: an elevator aboard, a restaurant with an ala carte menu from the Ritz-Carlton of London, and the main dining saloon used small tables instead of long tables. The ship measured 22,225 gross tons. The *AMERIKA* was the last major ship built for Germany in a British yard. The ship was big, not fast, with a speed of 17.5 knots.

Staten Island Municipal Ferry Boat "Manhattan" (Maiden Trip).

Publisher: National News Company, New York, NY, Card No. 7736 • Manufacturer: Printed In Leipzig, Germany • Type Color PolyChrome Photograph • Postmark: Not Used • Value Index: B

For many city dwellers, ferryboats are the first, and sometimes only, type of boats they know. Many New Yorkers have enjoyed a variety of fine ferry services. A premier route has been between Staten Island and the Battery, NY. Some evidence of this route's importance is the size of the ships on the Hudson River. The ferryboat *MANHATTAN* was a typical, big, comfortable double-ender. This vessel was new in 1905 and was owned by the City of New York. A crew of only 15 men was required for the 30-minute run. Built at Sparrows Point, MD, the ship measured 1,954 gross tons, length of 246 feet, and a beam of 46 feet. The craft's 3,500 horsepower engines provided a speed of 14 knots. Note the two odd-styled air funnels projecting from the base of the two smokestacks.

This photograph was made on the ferry's maiden trip, perhaps accounting for the large crowd of people on the upper deck and all the pennants. A many-paned glass skylight can be seen between the stacks. The twin round pilot houses were distinctive because of their slanted roofs each capped with a tall decorative lamp.

This Postcard is of significance to the author. It was written by the Newport, RI historian W. K. Covell, a man of many talents and an authority on the history of the famed Fall River Line. The *PROVIDENCE* was the Fall River Line's next-to-last large overnight boat. Known as the "Great White Queen" this steamer was constructed in 1905 at Quincy, MA. The vessel's top deck house covered almost the entire length of the steamer, similar to the top structure on the *COMMONWEALTH*. The ship was 4,365 gross tons, 279 feet long, a width of 50 feet, and a crew of 240 people which is indicative of the fine ser-

Publisher: Not Indicated • Manufacturer: Not Indicated • Type: Black-White Dull Finish Photograph • Postmark: Newport, RI, Januray 25, 1960 • Value Index E

vice for the 1,000 overnight passengers. The vessel's 5,500 horsepower engines permitted a speed of 18 knots on one of the nation's busiest waterways. The *PROVIDENCE* was sold for scrap in 1937.

This is a most unusual picture. It shows a wreck that occurred near Block Island. The steamer is the *SPARTAN*, of the Windsor Line, that ran from Providence, RI to New York City. The stranding of the ship occurred on March 17, 1905, with the photograph taken during the following day. When the photograph was taken, the ship was so badly battered that much of the wooden superstructure had already been washed off the hull. The one tall stack was gone and the main top mast had fallen off to the port side. Another mast was tilting and the waves would soon eliminate the remainder of the ship.

The steamer had run

Wreck of Steamer "Spartan" (March 18th, 1905), Block Island, R. J.

Publisher: Not Indicated • Manufacturer; Made In Germany • Type; Colored Dull Finish Photograph • Postmark: Providence, RI, August 10, 1908 • Value Index: D

aground in a bad snowstorm and was a total loss. Coastal steamers were vital to everyday life in those days and when one was wrecked it was important news. This Postcard must have been issued immediately after the wreck and was mailed to Lala Burr of Wickford, RI. The Windsor Line was absorbed by the Merchants & Miners Company shortly after the wreck.

This illustration shows the tragic wreck of the *HARVARD* that occurred at 3:00 AM on May 30, 1921. The *HARVARD* and the *YALE* were glamorous sisterships built in 1906 and 1907, respectively, by the Delaware River International Shipbuilding & Engine Works, Chester, PA. Based on design plans created by W. Denny & Brothers, of Dumbarton, Scotland the ships were different from the American-designed coastal steamers. Each had turbine propulsion and were triple screw steamers. Both ships were converted to burn oil instead of coal at three years of age and were pioneers in this conversion.The ships were 407 feet long, 61 feet wide,

Publisher: Steamship Historical Society of America • Manufacturer: Not Indicated • Type: Black-White Glossy Photograph • Postmark: Not Used • Value Index: E

10,000 horsepower, and could make 23 knots. Each ship had a crew of 135 people. They were built for the overnight run between New York City and Boston, MA. They operated on this route for three years and were sold for service on the West Coast. Their new run was between Los Angeles and San Francisco, CA.In World War I the *HARVARD* was called the *CHARLES* during troopship service. After the war ended, the ship returned to the Pacific Ocean and was rebuilt. The engines were raised to 14,000 horsepower.

HUDSON RIVER DAY LINE STEAMER "HENDRICK HUDSON".

Publisher: Hudson River Day Line • Manufacturer: Albertype Company, Brooklyn, NY • Type: Sepia Dull Finish Photograph • Postmark: Not Used • Value Index: F

People jammed the shoreline all along the Hudson River beginning at New York City to wave at the new *HENDRICK HUDSON* when this Hudson River Day Line excursion boat headed up toward Albany, NY in 1906. As the steamer approached the state capital, hundreds of people packed Kingston Park to wave torches, fire skyrockets, and build bonfires to welcome the new Hudson River Day Line beauty. This steamer, operated until 1948 with great success, measured 2,847 gross tons, was 390 feet long, and had a beam of 82 feet.

The *HUDSON* was constructed at Newburgh, NY by the T.S. Marvel SB Company. The hull was launched March 31, 1906, and towed to W. & A. Fletcher Company's plant at Hoboken, NJ to have six boilers and machinery installed. First trials were run August 18 and the new vessel made more than 23 miles an hour (knots were not used in this instance). The ship had 6,200 horsepower. Four open decks permitted the Day Liner to carry 5,000 passengers. It was often said that one-half of the children brought up in New York City knew this steamer as a close friend. Many people cried when the beautiful *HENDRICK HUDSON* was scrapped in 1951.

This illustration shows the *COLUMBIA*, (ex-*PRESIDENT*) built in 1907 at the New York SB Company, Camden, NJ. The *PRESIDENT* was built for service along the Pacific Coast under the Pacific SS Co. house flag. Other ships in the fleet had similar names: *CONGRESS, GOVERNOR,* and *SENATOR*.

As originally built, the *PRESIDENT* measured 5,453 gross tons, had a length of 417 feet, and a beam of 48 feet. There were 125 people in the crew. With 5,000 horsepower the steamer could do 14 knots. In July 1914 the *PRESIDENT* was converted to burn oil. In

P-444   S.S. Columbia - Inside Passage, Alaska

Publisher: Not Indicated • Manufacturer: EKC • Type: Black-White Glossy Photograph • Postmark: Not Used • Value Index: D

1922, the liner was acquired by the owner of the Admiral Line, H.F. Alexander. The *PRESIDENT* was his largest ship he decided to rename the vessel after his daughter. On the day the daughter was married, the *PRESIDENT* was rechristened *DOROTHY ALEXANDER* and the *San Francisco Chronicle*'s headline read: "GIRL LOSES NAME; GIVES IT TO A STEAMER."

In 1938 the *DOROTHY ALEXANDER* was given another name, *COLUMBIA*, when she was sold to the Alaskan Line. Finally, in 1946, the *COLUMBIA* was purchased by the Empresa de Navegacao Mercante Line of Portugal and renamed PORTUGAL. After six years of Portuguese service the ship was scrapped in 1952 at Spezia, Italy.

Some years ago the son of an old friend in Washington, D.C., called the author to say that his father was closing his office. Among the pictures on the walls was Antonio Jacobsen's original painting of the Mallory Line's *BRAZOS*, built in 1907 at Newport News, VA. This illustration is this same ship after the vessel had been renamed *SAN LORENZO*.

As originally built, the steamer had two black smokestacks, two tall masts and a superstructure stretching all the way aft. Measuring 418 feet in length and 54 feet in beam, the vessel had 6,576 gross tons. In 1916 Mallory sold the ship to the Porto Rico Line

STEAMSHIP "SAN LORENZO"   PORTO RICO LINE

Publisher: Porto Rico Line • Manufacturer: Albertype Company, Brooklyn, NY • Type: Black-White Dull Finish Photograph • Postmark: Not Used • Value Index: D

(original spelling). The vessel operated for four years, then was rebuilt and named *SAN LORENZO*. After World War I, the ship was again rebuilt, becoming an oil burner. The work included equipping the ship with wireless and reducing the passenger capacity to a total of 200 people. Thesuites cost $270 for the run to Puerto Rico. The liner did well all through the 1920s, but in 1934 was sold to Paolo Traves of Trieste, and taken there to be scrapped.

Built by the Bath Iron Works, Bath, ME in 1907 and 1909, the twin flyers *CAMDEN* and *BELFAST* were among the finest and fastest steamers on the Maine Coast. They ran between Bangor, ME and Boston, MA for the Eastern Steamship Company until 1936 when they were bought and renamed by the Colonial Line. The *CAMDEN* became the *COMET*. The *BELFAST* was renamed the *ARROW*. They were both built with turbine propulsion and triple screws. At 4,500 horse-power the ships were able to travel at 19 knots. Each ship mea-sured 2,153 gross tons, a length of 330 feet, and a beam of 58 feet. Each

Yankee Flagships ARROW and COMET are twin 19 knot ships, 330 ft. long with all steel hulls, powered by 4500 H. P. triple screw turbine engines.

Captain NORMAN L. STRICKLAND commanding S. S. COMET. Deckhand at 15; Ship's Master at 23; Captain famous Fall River Liner "Commonwealth" at 40.

COLONIAL LINE

Publisher: Colonial Line • Manufacturer: Not Indicated • Type: Blue Tone Dull Finish Photograph • Postmark: Not Used • Value Index: F

ship had twin stacks and three passenger decks. The Colonial Line issued at least six different types of Postcards for these fine ships. Three different funnel markings were shown on the various Postcards. The Colonial Line was doing its best to attract attention to their Long Island Sound overnight run in the dying days of American steamboating, pre-World War II. They operated from Providence, RI to New York City after the Fall River Line had stopped operat-ing. Both ended their careers doing heroic service as inter-island troopships in World War II.

This illustration shows a long-lived ship that served in World Wars I and II. The vessel was origi-nally built as a freighter and named *MAS-SACHUSETTS*. Then the ship was rebuilt as a high-speed passenger steamer. In World War I the vessel was taken over by the United States Government, rebuilt to become a mine layer, and renamed the *SHAWMUT*. After many years of Navy service the steamer was again rebuilt and renamed the *OGLALA*, for use in World War II as a seaplane tender. The vet-eran ship was at Pearl Harbor in December 1941 and survived the Japanese air attack. She measured 4,779 gross tons, a length of 375 feet, and a beam of 52 feet. With her two sisters,

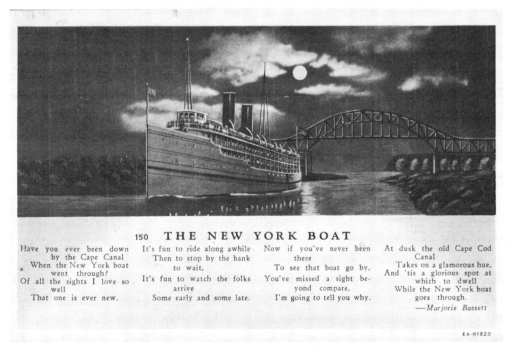

150 **THE NEW YORK BOAT**

Have you ever been down by the Cape Canal When the New York boat went through? Of all the sights I love so well That one is ever new.

It's fun to ride along awhile Then to stop by the bank to wait, It's fun to watch the folks arrive Some early and some late.

Now if you've never been there To see that boat go by, You've missed a sight be-yond compare, I'm going to tell you why.

At dusk the old Cape Cod Canal Takes on a glamorous hue, And 'tis a glorious spot at which to dwell While the New York boat goes through.
—*Marjorie Bassett*

6A-H1820

Publisher: E.D. West Company, S. Yarmouth, Cape Cod, MA • Manufacturer: C.T. Art-Colortone, Curt Teich & Company, Inc., Chicago, IL • Type: Colored Dull Finish Artist Conception • Postmark: Orleans, MA, September 3, Value Index D

the *BUNKER HILL* and the *OLD COLONY*, the *MASSACHUSETTS* initially operated between New York City and Boston, MA carrying cargo at high speed. The ship could make 20 knots, a high speed for freighters at that time. In this illustration the MASSACHUSETTS is shown rebuilt as a passenger ship and passing through the Cape Cod Canal in moonlight. The ship was abandoned in 1972 at age 65.

"The Ship with Superior Service" is how this liner was advertised on the back of the Postcard illustrated above. The GOVERNOR was new in 1907, having been built at Camden, NJ by the New York Shipbuilding Corporation for service between Seattle, WA and San Diego, CA under the house flag of the Pacific SS Company. The vessel measured 5,250 gross tons, with a length of 412 feet, a beam of 48 feet, and could accommodate 5,467 passengers. As originally built the steamer had two very tall stacks placed a little forward of the center. Shortly before World War I the GOVERNOR was

Publisher: Pacific Coast Steamship Company • Manufacturer: Not Indicated • Type: Black-White Dull Finish Photograph • Postmark: Not Used • Value Index: D

rebuilt and the masts were shortened. The GOVERNOR was well patronized until April 1, 1921. A collision with the freighter WEST HARTLAND, a much larger ship, brought the short career of the GOVERNOR to a close. The cargo ship struck the passenger liner on the starboard side. The vessel sank in 220 feet of water. Three passengers and three crew members died as a result of the accident. Decades later divers went down in search of $1,500,000 in gold and jewelry thought be aboard; they did not find anything.

This illustration shows another long-lived American coastal steamer. The HAVANA was built in 1907 for the Ward Line by William Cramp & Sons, of Philadelphia, PA. The HAVANA began life with two stacks and was rebuilt later with only one stack. The ship's basic dimensions remained the same: 6,678 gross tonnage, 429 feet in length, and a beam of 50 feet. With triple expansion engines and twin screws the steamer could make 17 knots. During World War I, the Ward liner became a hospital ship, renamed COMFORT for this duty.

The ship was again purchased by Ward,

Publisher: Southern Bell Telephone and Telegraph Company, Inc • Manufacturer: Not Indicated • Type: Photograph • Postmark: Not Used • Value Index: E

renamed HAVANA, rebuilt, and returned to the New York City to Havana, Cuba run. The grounding of the ship in 1934 brought front page attention to the old ship because it followed shortly after the burning of the line's flagship-the-almost-new MORRO CASTLE. The HAVANA was renamed YUCATAN and she sank at a New York City pier in 1940. The ship was raised and rehabilitated for United States Army transport work for World War II as the AGWILEON. In 1943 the name was changed to SHAMROCK and she was rebuilt as an Army hospital ship as shown in this illustration. The vessel was decommissioned in late 1945, and 15 years later she was towed to Hong Kong and scrapped.

This extraordinary steamship had seven names, five different careers, and, with her sistership, was the only modern liner to have six masts. The *REPUBLIC* is how the great steamship was known for the longest period. With 18,072 gross tonnage, this steamer was 615 feet long and had a beam of 68 feet.

In 1903 the vessel was launched as the *SERVIAN* by Harland & Wolff for J.P. Morgan's Leyland Line. This contract was cancelled and the unfinished steamer lay idle until purchased by the Hamburg American Line. Their initial plan was to name the big ship the *BROOKLYN* then the *CHICAGO* and *GEORGE WASHINGTON*. This latter name was abandoned when the North German Lloyd Line had a new liner called *GEORGE WASHINGTON*. Finally, *PRESIDENT GRANT* was selected and this name stayed for the remainder of the time as a German liner. The ship could carry 1,231 passengers in Steerage, 227 passengers in First Class, and 256 passengers in Second Class. The six masts were to hold cargo booms that served 11 cargo hatches. After World War I service as a transport under the United States flag the *GRANT* was renamed *PRESIDENT BUCHANAN* and then *REPUBLIC*, this last and seventh name was retained for the remaining 29 years of the ship's life. As a U.S. Lines passenger steamship the *REPUBLIC* often carried over 1,000 passengers. Also, the vessel did very poorly during three eastbound crossings in 1928 when fewer than 100 passengers were aboard on each trip. The United States Army operated the ship between 1931 and 1952.

Publisher: United American Lines, Card No. 3734 • Manufacturer: M & J •
Types: Sepia Tone Drawing • Postmark: Not Used • Value Index: D

Publisher: New England Steamship Company • Manufacturer: Not Indicated •
Type: Colored Drawing Poster • Postmark: Not Used • Value Index: D

The *CLEVELAND* is another of that large fleet of German liners trapped in American ports when World War I began. All of them were seized and used as United States troopships in the conflict. The *CLEVELAND*, which had belonged to the Hamburg American Line (HAPAG), was renamed *MOBILE*. The two-stacked beauty was built in 1908 with the plan of an around the world service for the ship.

Hapag president Albert Ballin was planning for the day when the Panama Canal would be completed. He was so enthusiastic that he could not wait for the waterway to be finished. With the new *CLEVELAND* he offered American travelers what he advertised as "Round-The-World" cruises with free connecting rail services across the United States back to their homes or point of departure just as many cruise lines do today. On one cruise the *CLEVELAND* would leave New York City and steam Eastward around the globe, ending at San Francisco, CA where the ship's passengers would be taken home by luxurious transcontinental trains. Then the liner would sail westward and end up in New York City, again with all expenses home by rail included. The fare for the 125-day world trip began at $800.

During the war, the *MOBILE* carried as many as 5,200 soldiers per trip to France. The ship's dimensions were: 16,900 gross tonnage, length 587 feet, and beam 65 feet. After World War I the *MOBILE* was transferred to Greek shipping interests and renamed *KING ALEXANDER* for operation between Piraeus, Greece and New York City.

Unfortunately, the operators failed in their business and the vessel, one of the most elegant and luxurious of the seized German liners, was acquired by W. Averill Harriman for his new United American Line, soon to become known as the Harriman Line. He gave the steamer the original name of *CLEVELAND*. Because of Prohibition that was in force at that time, Harriman found that he would be unable to sell liquor on his ships. After a brief attempt at a nonalcoholic American flag operation in the highly competitive Atlantic trade, he decided to end his experiment with shipping and sold his fleet to the Hamburg American Line. The circle was completed and Hapag regained the control of their lovely *CLEVELAND*. The steamer was used under the German flag on the Atlantic service, and scrapped in Germany in 1933, an early end for such a beautiful liner.

The *COMMONWEALTH*, new in 1908, was the last of the Fall River Line steamers. With 5,980 gross tons, a length of 456 feet, and a beam of 90 feet, this vessel had a proud appearance. One factor indicating the stature of the *COMMONWEALTH* was the 12,000 horsepower to drive the Fall River flagship between New York City and Fall River, RI every night. The steam pressure of her 10 boilers was 153 pounds-per-square inch, all of which permitted a speed of 22 knots. Only four other American steamboats exceeded the *COMMONWEALTH* in size the *SEEANDBEE*, *CITY OF DETROIT III*, *GREATER DETROIT*, and *GREATER BUFFALO*.

The *COMMONWEALTH* was built in Philadelphia, PA and was America's largest sidewheeler operating on salt water. The vessel had many new features which were advances over the older Fall River "Palace Steamers." One was the lack of masts, although there were nine flag staffs, one big enough to be thought of as a mast. It can be seen directly in front of the two tall black smokestacks in the photograph.

The shadow under the guards illustrates how the full width of the steamer's superstructure extended well out beyond the basic steel hull. The *COMMONWEALTH*'s paddle wheels were entirely enclosed and false stateroom windows covered the area where the old paddle box decorations would have been. After a short career, the flagship of the Fall River Line was made idle in 1937 by a long labor dispute and scrapped in 1938 at Baltimore, MD. The back side of the Postcard offers a final tribute to this remarkable vessel:

"To go from New York to Boston on a Fall River Line steamer is something more than embarking on a comfortable hotel late in the afternoon, sleeping soundly in blown sea air on a level keel all night, and reaching your destination in the morning clean and refreshed. It is an adventure in beauty."

The Hudson River Day Line steamer *ROBERT FULTON* was built in 1909 by the New York SB Corporation, Camden, NJ. This steamer was distinctive with three tall stacks. The *ROBERT FULTON* measured 2,168 gross tons, had a crew of 65, a length 346 feet, and a beam 76 feet. The ship was able to move at 20 miles per hour using 3,850 horsepower. The company used this method of describing the vessel's speed as they assumed this speed rating could be better understood by the general public. The *FULTON* ran continuously from 1909 through 1954, when the old vessel was laid up. The *FULTON* was

Publisher: Not Indicated, Card No. XXI • Manufacturer: Detroit Publishing Company • Type: Phostint Colored Photograph, Postmark: Yonkers...(Not legible) • Value Index: F

sold for conversion to a community center in the Bahamas in 1956. In 1964 Donald Ringwald, author of the authoritative book on the Day Line, noted that the *ROBERT FULTON* continued to be used for this purpose.

Among a choice of four almost identical potential Postcard illustrations for the *S.S. ALABAMA* something in all of the illustrations was obvious as peculiar to the Great Lakes. The position of the ship's name on the bow was strikingly different. The large letters of the name were very low, even below the heavy, rounded rub strake (the strong bumper-type strip of rounded steel placed just where the hull usually comes in contact with the dock). The name was only a few feet above the waterline. On coastal or ocean steamers the names are located forward near the top of the hull. Placing the name in a low position was obviously a Great Lakes tradition. One of the Postcards shows a broadside view of the

Publisher: Goodrich Steamship Lines • Manufacturer: T.C. Company, Chicago, IL • Type: Colored Glossy Photograph • Postmark: Not Used • Value Index: E

ship on the port side. Five large open cargo ports are shown on the deck above the rub strake.

Two of the four Postcards were published by the *ALABAMA*'s last owner, the Goodrich SS Line. The writing on the back of the Postcard chosen to be illustrated says: "Delightful Cruises to Picturesque *GEORGIAN BAY, GREEN BAY, MACKINAC AND THE SOO* — Many Short trips to Resorts and in Michigan and Wisconsin." The *ALABAMA* was built at Manitowoc, WI in 1910 and had a length of 250 feet, a beam of 44 feet, and 2,627 gross tonnage.

This Postcard of the *CITY OF ST. LOUIS* built in 1910, was made from a painting commissioned by the Savannah Line. The artist was not indicated on the Postcard. The small gaff-rigged sailing craft shown at the lower left was as good as a signature. One painter, Worden Wood, nearly always included a small craft in his liner portraits. This Postcard was doubtless offered free aboard ships of the company. The *CITY OF ST. LOUIS* was Hull No. 108 of the Newport News SB & DD Company, Newport News, VA. Hull No. 127 was a sistership, the *CITY OF MONTGOMERY*. Both served in World War I. The two ships were changed

Ocean S. S. Co. of Savannah—"SAVANNAH LINE"—S. S. City of St. Louis

Publisher: Savannah Line • Manufacturer: Not Indicated • Type Sepia Tone Painting • Postmark: Not Used • Value Index: E

to cargo ship status for World War II. Although the ships survived they were scrapped soon after World War II was over. The twin steamers each measured 5,425 gross tons, with a length of 271 feet and a beam of 49.7 feet. They had 2,300 horsepower and each required 77 in the crew.

This Postcard was produced using one of several thousand photographs made by the United States Army Signal Corps which formed the basis of the Steamship Historical Society of America Photographic Bank.

The *MADISON* was one of the smallest merchant ships used in World War II as a transport, part of a fleet of 16 ships operated as inter-island troop carriers in the Pacific. A careful examination will note that the deck house forward is still missing; it was lost in a hurricane on August 23, 1933. The *MADISON* was Hull No. 136 built at Newport News, VA. This Old Dominion Line steamer

S/S Madison

Publisher: Steamship Historical Society of America • Manufacturer: U.S. Army Signal Corps, Port of Embarkation, NY • Type: Glossy Photograph • Postmark: Not Used • Value Index: E

had 3,734 gross tons, 353 feet long, and a beam of 42 feet, 3,800 horsepower, and 80 people in the crew. The ship was built in 1911 and began a 36-year career that ended when the ship was sunk during 1912 in Chesapeake Bay. The ship was raised and put back into service, and became the *USS WARSZAWA* in honor of the new country of Poland formed after World War I. This little steamer operated in the Gulf of Mexico and the Caribbean. In 1923 the original owners repurchased the ship, restored the name *MADISON* to the bow, and returned the veteran to the run between Virginia and New York City. This time the MADISON had 15 years of continuous service until the beginning of World War II ended the steamer's operations. Again, the MADISON was placed in war service and retained the same name. After the war the old ship was laid up in Boston, MA and scrapped at Providence, RI in 1947.

The *SANKATY* was built in 1911 and not scrapped until 1964, a long life. A product of the Fore River SB Company Yard, Quincy, MA, this 195-foot long vessel had a beam of 36 feet and measured 1,871 gross tons. The *SANKATY* was the only ferry on the Martha's Vineyard, MA and Nantucket, RI run to have two smokestacks. After an extensive fire in 1924, the little vessel was sold and refurbished for operation between Port Jefferson, NY and Bridgeport, CT. In the rebuilding of the ship the original engine room casing, warped and bent in the fire, was retained, partially hidden by a new outer steel bulkhead. After

Steamer "Sankaty" at Wharf.   Oak Bluffs, Mass.

Publisher: Fred H. Perry, Oak Bluffs, MA • Manufacturer: The Albertype Company, Brooklyn, NY • Type: Colored Dull Finish Photograph • Postmark: Not Used • Value Index: E

rebuilding, the veteran steamer ran for a short time on the Oyster Bay, NY to Stamford, CT route. In 1940, the ship was sold to Northumberland Ferrier, Ltd., Charlottetown, Prince Edward Island, Canada, for use in the Bay of the St. Lawrence. The name was changed to *CHARLES A. DUNNING* sometime during this period, but the handsome two-stack silhouette was never altered.

This illustration shows the *CITY OF DETROIT III*, built in 1912. This, while exaggerated, is the finest steamboat painting of a Great Lakes passenger ship ever done. It was used in many ways on brochures, letterheads, steamer artifacts such as menus. The owners of the Detroit & Cleveland Navigation Company quickly realized the value of this painting for publicity purposes. In advertisements they offered the public an opportunity to own a print of a similar painting "Now Come Still Evening On" for $1.00 postpaid. The

City of Detroit, Ill., Between Cleveland and Buffalo.

Publisher: Not Indicated • Manufacturer: Not Indicated • Type: Colored Painting • Postmark: Not Used • Value Index: F

statistics for the *CITY OF DETROIT III* were breathtaking: 8,800 sheets, 4,050 pieces of silverware, etc. The safety features included lifeboats and rafts for all passengers plus 4,200 life preservers, an automatic sprinkling system, thermostat fire alarm system, 11 watertight compartments, fire and boat drill twice a week and "50% more life saving equipment than required." The steamer's dimensions: 6,061 gross tons, 455 feet in length, 55 foot beam, and 9,000 horsepower. When the ship was scrapped the Gothic Room, with its ornate oak carving, paintings, and huge stained glass window was saved. This choice artifact eventually was given to the Dossin Great Lakes Museum, Detroit, MI. Some 2,000 souvenir hunters boarded the steamer before the scrapping to buy pitchers, platters, tableware, and anything with the Detroit & Cleveland Navigation Company logo on it.

S. S. PASTORES ~ *Colombian Line*

New York - Haiti - Jamaica - Colombia, So. Am. - Panama Canal

Publisher: Columbia Line • Manufacturer: Not Indicated • Type: Gray Tones Photograph • Postmark: Not Used •
Value Index: D

The United Fruit Company had a large fleet of passenger-carrying banana steamers. Although many were built abroad and run under foreign flags because of the high cost of American operation, they were thought of as American ships. The largest ships of the pre-World War I era were the *CALAMARES, TENADORES* and *PASTORES*, built in 1912 and known as "The Elite Three." The *TENADORES* was lost in World War I. The other two ships continued through World War II.

This illustration shows the *PASTORES* during a period when the usually all-white steamer was on charter to the Columbian Line. All three of these steamers were built by Workman Clark & Company of Belfast, Ireland. The *CALAMARES* measured 7,782 gross tons, was 470 feet long, and had a 55-foot beam. With twin screws and quadruple expansion engines the ship could make 15 knots. Excellent passenger accommodations were offered for 143 persons. The steamer ran on various routes linking the east coast of the United States with Central America until the 1950s, when they were sold for scrap.

Another steamer that was the last of a specialized type was the Hudson Navigation Company's *BERKSHIRE*. The company was known as the Hudson River Night Line. The ship was the culmination of 106 years of bigger and better ships. The *BERKSHIRE* was the evolutionary high point in overnight boats on the Hudson River. She was the last of the famous night boats serving between New York City and Albany, NY, and no more of these steamers were built before World War II as the automobile had the public esteem. Five passenger decks with every available luxury of

164   Hudson River at Night, New York City

Publisher: Frank E. Cooper, 258 Broadway, New York, NY, Card No. 164-7A-H3775 • Manufacturer: Curt Teich &
Company, Chicago, IL • Type: C.T. Art-Colortone • Postmark: Not Used • Value Index: E

the day were offered. The *BERKSHIRE* was built in 1913 by New York SB Corporation, Camden, NJ. With a 4,500 gross tonnage, the ship had a length of 440 feet and a beam of 50 feet. The steam pressure of her boilers was only 83 pounds-per-square inch, for speed was not important on this overnight route. As the Economic Depression dampened the nation's economy in the early 1930s, the service was abandoned in 1939, and the *BERKSHIRE* was laid up. In 1941 she was sold for $65,000 to the United States Government and towed to Bermuda for use as a barracks.

Publisher: Aratusa Supper Club, Secaucus, NJ • Manufacturer: Not Indicated • Type: Colored Oversize Photograph • Postmark: Not Used • Value Index: E

HUDSON RIVER DAY LINE STEAMER "DE WITT CLINTON."

Publisher: Hudson River Day Line • Manufacturer: The Albertype Company, Brooklyn,NY • Type: Sepia Toned Photograph • Postmark: Not Used • Value Index: E

Built originally as the *RANGELEY*, this jaunty little steamer was designed for ferry service from a railhead, to Bar Harbor, Mount Desert Island, ME. The vessel, constructed in 1913 at the Bath Iron Works for the Maine Central Railroad, carried many of the elite and famous to their homes along the coast of Maine. A single screw, steel hulled, three decker, the 652 gross ton *RANGELEY* was 185 feet long, 35 feet wide, and had a 1,100 passenger capacity. The steamer could make 18 knots.

Purchased in 1925 by the Hudson River Day Line, the little vessel began a second career with a new name. Alfred Van Sanfort Olcott, long time owner of the Day Line, thought it would be nice to honor the U.S. Senator from New York, Chauncey M. Depew, while he was still living and could appreciate it. Olcott called Depew on his 91st birthday and told him there would be a Day Liner named after him. An oil painting of Senator Depew by Orlando Rouland was commissioned and it was hung in the ship's main saloon. The *CHAUNCEY M. DEPEW* made excursions out of New York or wherever needed. In World War II the vessel was purchased by the War Shipping Administration for $101,000 and it passed out of Day Line control.

The ship was sold again at the end of the war. The steamer served for some time as a tender for liners too large to dock at Bermuda. The steamer became a restaurant on the Hackensack River, NJ, a short-lived service that ended when the vessel sank at its pier.

The vagaries of fate are amazing. There were two excellent sisterships built for a service that had plenty of money behind it and every reason to anticipate success. The pair of ships were part of a dream by Charles M. Hayes, president of the Grand Trunk Railroad. He planned to run a rail-steamer line from Montreal, Canada to New York City. The sisterships provided the water link from Providence, RI to Manhattan, NY. Hayes selected the best known American-naval architect of the day, Frank E. Kirby, who designed these twin overnight steamers to be large, fast and luxurious. The two ships were the *MANHATTAN* and the *NARRAGANSET*, built in 1913 by Harland & Hollingsworth, Wilmington, DE. They were of steel, with twin screws, and measured 3,899 gross tons. Each was 332 feet long, 66 feet wide, and had 4,000 horsepower with a top speed of 23 knots.

Neither ship was on the projected route. After a long period of idleness the *MANHATTAN* served in the early maritime history of Israel. All of these changes occurred because of one fact. Hayes took passage on a ship named *TITANIC*. He was lost and his dream died with him. World War I provided them with a new life. They were acquired by the United States Navy and steamed to Europe for cross-channel troopship service. The *MANHATTAN* was renamed *NOPATIN*. The *NARRAGANSET* eventually returned to the United States and was sold to Canada SS Company to serve for many years as the overnight cruising steamship *RICHELIEU*. The Hudson River Day Line bought the ex-*MANHATTAN*. Renamed *DE WITT CLINTON*, the war weary steamer was rebuilt to carry 5,000 people as a day excursion boat, entering this service on May 12, 1921. This illustration shows the vessel while on the Hudson River. World War II saw the steamer renamed the *COL. FREDERICK C. JOHNSON* as a United States troopship. In 1947 the ship was purchased by Samuel Derecktor to move the Jewish people from the various wartime concentration camps to a new homeland in Palestine. The steamer was renamed the *DERECKTOR*. Sailing for the Mediterranean, the boat was renamed again, becoming the *GALILAH*, The ship was operated under the house flag of the Zim Shipping Company and was advertised as "A 3,800-ton steamer able to carry up to 1,000 immigrants and a restricted number of cabin class passengers" to the new State of Israel. The *GALILAH* was out of date and was finally sold for scrap in 1953.

Publisher: Hiawatha Card of Detroit, Card No. P25364 • Manufacturer: Colouspicture Publishers, Inc., Boston, MA •
Type: Plastichrome • Postmark: Not Used • Value Index: E

Publisher: Costa Line, Genova, Italy • Manufacturer: G. Schenone, Genova, Italy • Type:
Colored Photograph • Postmark: Not Used • Value Index: E

The NORTH AMERICAN (Left ship in the illustration) and the SOUTH AMERICAN were the last regularly scheduled steamers operating under an American flag on the Great Lakes. A high point in their careers was being selected as members of the parade when the St. Lawrence Seaway was officially opened by Queen Elizabeth and President Dwight D. Eisenhower in 1958. These two lovely white steamers followed the Royal Yacht BRITANNIA. They were positioned side by side and represented the United States. This honor was a high point in the long and colorful careers of these steamers. Unfortunately, the life of the ships did not end at this event as they each had a disaster.

The ships were owned by the Georgian Bay Lines during their 53 years of operation. They provided transportation between various lake ports. As cruising became more popular they were rebuilt with two stacks instead of one stack and enlarged with cruise ship facilities. They ran from Chicago, IL to Duluth, MN with "Outstanding passenger service, unsurpassed cuisine."

As labor costs increased, the NORTH AMERICAN was retired in 1962. The SOUTH AMERICAN continued alone in service for five additional years climaxing her service with eight round trips to Montreal, Canada during the EXPO 67. Sad endings came for the ships, one came quickly and totally unexpected and the other over a 20-year period. In mid-1967 the Seafarers International Union purchased the NORTH AMERICAN. They wanted her to be used as a dormitory at their training center for seamen located at Piney Point, MD. The 2,317 gross ton liner was turned over to a towing company for the passage without a riding crew aboard. The 290-foot long ship was at the end of a 1200-foot towline and it suddenly went down in 36 fathoms of water. The sea was moderate, however, no one was aboard to man the pumps. A small almost unnoticed leak in the ship was the cause. The crew of the towing tug was able to cut the line to prevent the ship from pulling the tug with it.

The Seafarers International Union immediately purchased the SOUTH AMERICAN and was able to complete the towing to Piney Point without further incident. The ship was used for a short time as a dormitory and then abandoned. She was moved in the late 1980s to the Kurt Iron & Metal Company Yard to be scrapped.

This ship is the oldest ocean-going passenger ship in the world. Under the steamer's current name, DOULOS, the 6,600 gross ton vessel is probably known by more people than any other ship afloat today. This illustration is of the ship in 1952 under the Costa Line house flag. Built in 1914 by the Newport News SB & DD Company, Newport News, VA, the ship began life as the MEDINA, a Mallory Line cargo ship, running between New York City and Texas. With a length of 421 feet and a beam of 55 feet, the MEDINA's 15 knots qualified the freighter as one of the fastest cargo ships.

After 34 years of service under the red-starred house flag of Mallory, the MEDINA was sold, renamed ROMA, to carry immigrants from Europe to Canada, Australia, and later Israel. In 1952 Giacomo Costa fu Andrea, owner of the famous Costa Line, acquired the vessel and renamed from the Costa family, the FRANCA C. Beneath all the outer evidence of glamor at sea such as outdoor pool, colorful deckchairs, and complete air conditioning was the 1914 hull of an American coastal cargo ship.

The ship ran between Italy and South America and did well. They continued to improve their "Old Man" as the little FRANCA C. was known within the firm.

In 1970 the MEDINA, then 56 years old, began a fourth career, sold to a nonprofit German Christian youth movement, Operation Mobilization. A new name, DOULOS, which loosely translated meant Slave of Jesus. To date the ship has continued to serve, sailing with a smaller ship named LOGOS on a modern-day missionary effort. A 1987 brochure published by the "Good Books for All" project reported that the two vessels had visited 87 countries and had been visited by seven million underprivileged people.

The *SEEANDBEE* was the only passenger ship on the Great Lakes to have four smokestacks. When finished in 1913, the owners advertised: "She is greater in cost, larger in all proportions, richer in all appointments than any steamer on inland waterways of the world." They gave the craft one of the most lack luster names that could have been given, *SEEANDBEE*. The name was suggested by the winner in a ship-naming contest and was picked because the ship was intended to run between Cleveland, OH (for the "See") and Buffalo, NY (for the "Bee").

This name also caused a problem. In 1925, when the largest ship in the world was the *LEVIATHAN*, a garbled radio message was picked up by the liner. The message seemed to have been sent from what sounded like "The great ship SEEANDBEE." The radio operator on the *LEVIATHAN* queried: "Please identify . . . the great ship . . . what?" Apparently the *SEEANDBEE*'s radio equipment had enough power that its messages could be heard far out on the Atlantic. They were too embarrassed to reply.

The *SEEANDBEE* was owned by the Cleveland & Buffalo Transit Company. and measured 6,381 gross tons, 500 feet long and 98.9 feet wide. This ship's 12,000 horsepower engines drove the *SEEANDBEE* at 22 miles per hour. The four stacks were nine feet in diameter. The ship was built at Wyandotte, MI, to outdo the *GREATER DETROIT III* of the Detroit and Cleveland Navigation Company.

The *SEEANDBEE* entered service on June 13, 1913, and a great deal of publicity was given to the fact that the new vessel was unsinkable and safe from fire. The ship had steel construction with an automatic sprinkler system. After a long career on Lake Erie the ship was converted into an aircraft carrier *WOLVERINE* in 1942. The ship was scrapped in 1947. The *SEEANDBEE* was elected to the American Merchant Marine Museum's National Maritime Hall of Fame in 1987.

The *WASHINGTON IRVING* was the largest steamer ever built for the Hudson River Day Line. The ship measured 3,104 gross tons and cost $838,000 when built in 1913. The construction was by the New York SB Co., Camden, NJ; the ship was 441 feet in length and 86 feet wide.

After a brief career the great white excursion steamer was sunk in 1926. Two passengers and one crew member were lost. The passengers were a mother and her three-year-old daughter who had waited too long on the lowest deck for two other children. The mother did not know the two children had been saved. The lost crew member was a mess boy who was trapped in a hold. The accident occurred near 129th St., New York City. The tug *THOMAS E. MORAN* was coming up river with two loaded oil barges one on either side of the tug. The tug had the right of way. After sounding a warning whistle the big Day Line steamer backed out from the pier and was unable to avoid hitting the barge. The *WASHINGTON IRVING* had a hole below the waterline and the 10-year old ship went down quickly. A year later the hull was raised, however, only the engine could be saved. The remainder of the ship had to be scrapped.

THE GREAT SHIP SEEANDBEE, DAILY BETWEEN CLEVELAND AND BUFFALO.

Publisher: George R. Klein News Company, Cleveland, OH • Manufacturer: TB, Cambridge, MA • Type: Colored Photograph Tichnor Quality Views • Postmark: Not Used • Value Index: F

ANTHONY'S NOSE AND HUDSON RIVER DAY LINE STEAMER "WASHINGTON IRVING"

Publisher: Hudson River Day Line • Manufacturer: The Albertype Company, Brooklyn, NY • Type: Sepia Toned Photograph • Postmark: Not Used • Value Index: F

United States Line S. S. "Leviathan" 59,956 Tons

Publisher: Not Indicated • Manufacturer: Not Indicated • Type: Glossy Photograph Oversize • Postmark: Not Used • Value Index: C

Publisher: Panama Pacific Line • Manufacturer: Not Indicated • Type: Black-White Dull Finish Photograph •
Postmark: Not Used • Value Index: D

The *LEVIATHAN* was built for the Hamburg American Line and began life as the *VATERLAND*. The *LEVIATHAN* was put into service in 1914, only months before World War I began. The ship was Albert Ballin's "Money on the line" to prove he was serious in his effort to dissuade the Kaiser from war with Great Britain. Unfortunately, the Kaiser's wife hated him because he was a Jew and isolated her husband from his influence letting the drums of war roll free. After only three and one-half round trips the *VATERLAND* found herself trapped by the British Navy in the New York City port. When America entered World War I the *VATERLAND* was seized and renamed *LEVIATHAN*. Converted to carry 14,000 troops in one trip, the huge vessel came to be known as "The Big Train," or the "Levi-Nathan." The troubles for the ship began in 1918. William Randolph Hearst eliminated the one company that might have succeeded in running the *LEVIATHAN* successfully. A new United States Lines was created but political control and the beginning of Prohibition further reduced the ship's ability to compete against established foreign liners. On occasions the American flagship carried more passengers than any other steamer; however, the U.S. Lines, the operator, continually lost money.

This ship was known for the first TV experiments aboard ship, the first symphony concert broadcast at sea, and use of the first ship-to-shore radio telephone. The efforts to make the steamship rated the world's fastest and the claim that the *LEVIATHAN* was the largest ship were destroyed by a money saving plan to cut port dues by reducing the stated gross tonnage. Also, one Congressman made himself world famous by denouncing the ship for using French words on the dinner menus.

Another unfavorable event occurred in a dense fog. The huge vessel was ordered by the Shipping Board to come in to New York City and the steamer ran aground causing Captain Herbert Hartley to be ridiculed as "Mud Turtle Hartley." The liner became the greatest white elephant of all time. The ship's sale for scrap prior to the beginning of World War II was a national calamity equal to the loss of the French superliner *NORMANDIE* by fire.

The story of the *BELGIC* or *BELGENLAND* began in 1914. World War I caused the half-finished ship to be given to White Star Line to operate as the *BELGIC*, using their traditional system of ending a name with "ic." At the end of the war, following a long period of indecision, the big craft was finally completed as the *BELGENLAND* and began sailing in April 1923. The steamer became best known for cruising. Dr. Albert Einstein escaped from Germany aboard the *BELGENLAND* on the vessel's sixth world cruise.

In 1931, because of the Economic Depression, the lovely three-stacked liner went from the sublime to the ridiculous by offering what were called "Booze Cruises" sailing out of New York City, as the nation girded itself to rescind Prohibition. A Daily News report on the first such cruise wrote that New York gangsters were outraged that some legitimate interests ``Had infringed on their business to the tune of $550,000 worth of serious drinking."

The *BELGENLAND* was transferred to American registry and the ship was operated in the coastal cruise trade with the new name of COLUMBIA. She failed in this new service and was scrapped in Scotland in 1936. The 27,132 gross ton liner had a length of 697 feet and a beam of 90 feet. This illustration shows the steamer flying the American flag while belonging to the Panama Pacific Line, a subsidiary of the J.P. Morgan combine.

The Great Lakes superships *NORTH WEST* and *NORTH LAND*, and the Pacific passenger-cargo twins *MINNESOTA* and *DAKOTA* have been described above. These vessels were four of James J. Hill's extraordinary ships. There are two other ships that will complete this description of the dramatic contribution to world shipping made by this railroad magnate. They were the *GREAT NORTHERN*, shown in the upper illustration, launched on July 7, 1914 and the *NORTHERN PACIFIC* shown in the lower illustration. Each ship was given the name of one railroad system owned by Hill. The

Publisher: Not Indicated • Manufacturer: Not Indicated • Type: Black-White Glossy Photograph • Postmark: Not Used • Value Index: D

two ships were designed to offer a sea connection with San Francisco, CA from Hill's Western rail terminal at Portland, OR. Retired Ship Chief Engineer John C. Carrothers described the *GREAT NORTHERN*: "Her long and eventful life was so packed with spectacular and glamorous incidents many believed 'Hot Foot' (this was the steamer's nickname later in life) was the greatest ship that ever sailed." These liners performed their job well, helping to get passengers to San Francisco, CA faster than those taking the more direct route from Chicago, IL to San Francisco by other railroad lines. The ships were known as the "Palaces of the Pacific." They remain at this writing the largest and fastest coastwise passenger steamers ever built in America. Their dimensions included 8,367 gross

Steamship Northern Pacific of the Great Northern Pacific Steamship Company, between San Francisco and Portland, Oregon, via Astoria

Publisher: Great Northern Pacific Steamship Company • Manufacturer: Not Indicated • Type: Colored Painting • Postmark: Not Used • Value Index: C

tons, 509 feet length, and 63 feet beam. Unfortunately, World War I drastically altered their activities. The *NORTHERN PACIFIC* ran aground near Saltaire on Fire Island, NY. The large number of wounded soldiers on board were all rescued and the ship pulled free. Damage to the ship was extensive. Shortly after, the ship burned and sank en route to the West Coast. Ship owner Alexander, who had purchased the *NORTHERN PACIFIC* then acquired the *GREAT NORTHERN*. The United States Navy had renamed this vessel *COLUMBIA*, transforming the ship into their Atlantic Fleet Flagship. Alexander went over the head of the Secretary of the Navy directly to President Harding and obtained the *GREAT NORTHERN* from the Navy amid extensive outcry in the press. He named his prize after himself using his initials and name. This story is the basis for the ship winning the nickname of "Hot Foot," the first letters H F" representing the first two initials of the name. As flagship of the Admiral Line the ship extended the fame for

(Continued on the next page)

the name H.F. Alexander. The steamer's speed required two captains, one relieving the other on each successive voyage between San Francisco and Los Angeles, CA. Currently the flyer often appears in old Hollywood films shown on TV, as the ship's proximity and glamour offered a natural movie set to film directors of that day. During World War II, the *H.F. ALEXANDER* was renamed *GENERAL GEORGE S. SIMONDS*. Another exploit of this steamship included being second in line of ships heading toward the beaches of Normandy, France on the day after D Day. When the *SUSAN B. ANTHONY*, first in line, was sunk, old "Hot Foot" took the lead, delivered all the troops and returned to England for additional troops.

After the war the ship regained the old name of *H.F. ALEXANDER* and was laid up in the James River, VA near the *PRESIDENT WARFIELD*, soon to become the EXODUS 1947. No one wanted the tired old "Palace of the Pacific" and in 1948 the ship's name was missing from the American Bureau of Shipping's list of active vessels. The H.F. *ALEXANDER* was scrapped by the Sun SB & DD Company at Chester, PA.

S/S Maui

Publisher: Steamship Historical Society of America • Manufacturer: Not Indicated • Type: Black-White Glossy Photograph • Postmark: Not Used • Value Index: D

Captain William Matson, Swedish-born American shipping genius, introduced four new passenger-cargo steamers between 1908 and 1917. All of the ships had their engines aft. This major engineering innovation, popularized by the MAUI, built in 1917, was not adopted until 1956 by any modern-day naval architect. In 1956, the Shaw, Savill & Albion Line's *SOUTHERN CROSS* was launched, with engines and stack at the stern.

The world's maritime press hailed the design as a striking innovation. This steamer continues to sail as the *AZURE SEAS* of the modern-day Admiral Line. The *MAUI* was a ship of 9,801 gross tons, 501 feet length, and had a 58-foot beam. A crew of 140 was required. The ship's 10,000 horsepower permitted a top speed of 16 knots. The ship had a cruising radius of 13,500 miles as required to cover the long Pacific routes of Matson Line. This extended range was ideal for world wide troopship service in the two World Wars. During World War I, this vessel was converted to carry 3,800 troops. In World War II the Army rebuilt the steamer to travel with only 1,650 troops per trip. Between the two wars the *MAUI* was restored to Matson peacetime service with "Many improvements."

This illustration shows a little liner built in 1915 in Holland by Kon. Maatsde Schelde, of Flushing, Holland. With two sisterships, this steamer was purchased in 1916 for trans-Pacific service by the Pacific Mail Line. This ship was named *ECUADOR*, while the sisterships were called the *COLOMBIA* and *VENE-ZUELA*. Each measured 5,544 gross tons, 380 feet long, and had a 48-foot beam. They were single screw steamers with a speed of 14 knots. Between 1915 and 1921 they made the run from San Francisco, CA to Hong Kong and Manila, Philippines. In 1937 the steamer was

Publisher: Panama Mail Steamship Company • Manufacturer: Swadley Photographist • Type: Black-White Glossy Photograph • Postmark: Not Legible • Value Index: D

sold and renamed *DAVID W. BRANCH*, a name the ship retained through troopship service during World War II. At the end of the war the *DAVID W. BRANCH* was acquired by Israel and renamed *LUXOR* and then finally *NEGBAH*, doing service in the Mediterranean. In May 1948, when the State of Israel was proclaimed, this ship was the largest of four passenger liners operating under the Israeli flag. The others were the *GALILAH*, *KEDMAH*, and *ARTSAH*. Israel was proud of the *NEGBAH*, as can be seen from this paragraph printed in an undated folder published in approximately 1950:"Largest of the Zim-Israel passenger vessels, the *NEGBAH* is admirably equipped for fast, thorough comfortable service."

Without question the *MINNEKAHDA* is one of the most interesting liners. Construction was interrupted by World War I. After the war, the *MIN-NEKAHDA* was converted to carry 2,000 passengers in steerage between Danzig, Poland, and New York City, as part of the American Line. The name showed the ship had been originally planned for use under the Atlantic Transport Line banner. All their ships had names starting with "Minne" such as the *MIN-NEHAHA* or the *MIN-NEWASKA*.

Operation by the American Line on the run from Danzig was not satisfactory and the vessel was rebuilt, this time with

Publisher: Atlantic Transport Line • Manufacturer: Not Indicated • Type: Colored Painting • Postmark: Not Used • Value Index: E

W. F. Gibbs as the naval architect. His had a new design and the *MINNEKAHDA* emerged as the first entirely Tourist Class ship on the Atlantic for the Atlantic Transport Co.

STEAMSHIPS "ORIZABA" AND "SIBONEY"

Publisher: Ward Line Mediterranean-Black Sea Service, McDonnell & Truda General Agents, New York, NY •
Manufacturer: Not Indicated • Type: Black-White Artist Conception • Postmark: Not Used • Value Index: B

U. S. HOSPITAL SHIP CHARLES A. STAFFORD
ARRIVES AT PORT OF EMBARKATION
CHARLESTON, S. C.

Photo by U. S. Army Signal Corps

Publisher: Southern Bell Telephone and Telegraph Company, Inc. • Manufacturer: Not Indicated • Type: Black-White
Dull Finish Photograph • Postmark: Not Used • Value Index: E

These two sisterships, shown on the preceding page, are an example of how some American coastal steamers were large enough to become regular ocean liners. The upper illustration is the Ward Line's *ORIZABA*, showing this vessel as a regular trans-Atlantic passenger ship operating between Black Sea ports and New York City. The ship was built for the company's premier run between New York City, Cuba, and the west coast of Mexico. The *ORIZABA* was capable of performing more than routine trips and proved it in World Wars I and II, completing her career as a Brazilian passenger ship named *DUQUE DE CAXIAS*. The lower illustration shows the *ORIZABA*'s sistership, the *SIBONEY*, while serving in World War II as the hospital ship *CHARLES A. STAFFORD*. The two ships were built by William Cramp & Sons SB Company, Philadelphia, PA in 1918.

Both ships were twin screw, 17-knot steamships measuring 6,938 gross tons. Looking at their outline they could have been considered medium-sized foreign deep-sea passenger ships. If they had been registered under a foreign flag their gross tonnage would have been close to 10,000 tons. All American gross tonnage figures provided in this book are from one-quarter to one-third less than the tonnage figures would have measured if they were operated under the flag of any of the other leading maritime nations of the world.

These ships were 443 feet long with a beam of 60 feet. As originally built they were designed to carry 306 passengers in First Class, 60 passengers in Second Class, and 64 passengers in Third Class. In basic outline the hull, superstructure, twin stacks, and two tall pole masts anticipate the look of the same company's two largest liners that were built in 1930, the ill-fated *MORRO CASTLE* and the *ORIENTE*. This concept supports the people who say that major ship lines do often establish a family look in the silhouette and style of their ships. The Ward Line's most famous naval architect was Theodore Ferris. He created the *MORRO CASTLE* and the *ORIENTE*. Does any reader know if he was the naval architect for the *ORIZABA* and the *SIBONEY*?

In 1939 the *ORIZABA* was in the newspaper headlines because of a charter by the United States government to bring back survivors of the British liner *ATHENIA*. The *ATHENIA* was the first major passenger ship torpedoed and sunk by the Germans in World War II. For this service a large American flag was painted on either side of the hull just forward of the first stack. As a World War II troopship, this vessel was rebuilt to carry 1,578 passengers and 35,455 cubic feet of cargo. The Ward Line went into bankruptcy shortly after the end of World War II and never regained either of these sisterships. The first ship lost was the *SIBONEY*, scrapped in 1957 after a long period of idleness. At this writing there is not any satisfactory evidence that the *DUQUE DE CAXIAS* has been scrapped.

The pair of ships shown on the next page sailed under eight different names, running in the Caribbean for Grace Line, between New York City and Baltimore, MD for the Merchants & Miners Company. Also, on world wide services for the United States Army and Navy, as a troopship and a hospital ship. Both ships were built by William Cramp & Sons, Philadelphia, PA in 1918. They have the strong family resemblance of the famous Grace Line, well decks forward, three promenade decks piled high, and a nicely centered single smokestack. The upper illustration shows the *JOHN L. CLEM* as an Army hospital ship serving out of Charleston, SC. The *JOHN L. CLEM* was scrapped in 1948.

The illustration below shows the ship sailing as the *KENT* under the Merchants & Miners house flag. The *KENT*'s last service was also as an Army hospital ship, the *ERNEST HINDS*. This little liner used the same name through 1957 when she was scrapped.

Grace Line ships were all given "Santa" names. Then the *SANTA ANA*'s name was changed to *GUATEMALA* for operation by the Panama Mail Line, a Grace subsidiary which operated on the line between San Francisco, CA and New York City. Later, the steamer was returned to the regular Grace fleet and again renamed, becoming the *SANTA CECILIA*. Grace was continually expanding and adding newer and larger ships. The *SANTA CECILIA* became surplus and was sold to the Merchants & Miners Line and received another name in the process, the *IRWIN*, befitting that famous company's naming system.

The *ERNEST HINDS* began her career as the Grace Line's *SANTA TERESA*. The Merchants & Miners Line also acquired this sistership and renamed her the *KENT*. This liner operated between Boston, MA and Richmond, VA, carrying up to 114 passengers and large quantities of freight. When war came, the *KENT* was taken over by the Army and converted for use as a transport, with accommodations for 751 passengers. At this time the ship was named *ERNEST HINDS*, in honor of Major General Ernest Hinds, who was Chief of Artillery, AEF, in World War I. The work of making the steamer into a transport was accomplished by the Bethlehem Steel Company yard in Boston, MA.

When given to the Navy, the ex-Grace liner began a long series of troop-carrying voyages in the Caribbean and the Pacific. At one point, the ship was chased by a Japanese submarine and grounded on a coral reef off Guadalcanal. Fortunately, there were no casualties and only slight damage to the ship. These fine little steamers measured 4,870 gross tons, 360 feet long, and had a beam of 51 feet. Their quadruple expansion engines provided 14 knots with a radius of 10,000 miles.

Publisher: Southern Bell telephone and Telegraph Company, Inc. • Manufacturer: Not Indicated • Type: Black-White Dull Finish Photograph • Postmark: Not Used • Value Index: E

Publisher:Not Indicated • Manufacturer: Not Indicated • Type: BGlossy Photograph • Postmark: Not Legible • Value Index: E

Occasionally a ship can be considered to have an almost human personality. The *SCANPENN* and the three other sisterships on the same service (*SCANYORK, SCANMAIL,* and *SCANSTATES*) are ships of this type. The ships were part of the American Scantic Line, a subsidiary of the once-great Moore McCormack Lines. At first glance looking at the illustration you may see only a small cargo ship. The abundance of cargo gear on the sturdy ship and the fore mast indicates the ship was a freighter. However, the colorful spread of signal flags means something quite different. Why would a cargo ship be dressed with so many code flags? And what about that new-looking, white, squared off superstructure?

The American Scantic quartet ran primarily as cargo ships between New York City and Scandinavian ports, thus the prefix "Scan" As rebuilt by the naval architect George Sharp, they each had remarkably fine passenger accommodations for 101 persons. The first sailing was during the Economic Depression, on June 11, 1932. They were among the slowest vessels on the Atlantic Ocean, requiring 12 days to reach Copenhagen, Denmark and they were the "Bargain of the Atlantic." According to the maritime scholar, Mark Goldberg. All cabins were outside, with private facilities, making them unique on the Atlantic Ocean. The four "Scan" ships were built in 1919 as freighters by the American International SB Corporation, Hog Island, PA. Each measured 5,152 gross tons, 390 feet long, and had a beam of 54 feet.

Publisher: American Scantic Line • Manufacturer: C.T. Art-Colortone by Alfred Robbins, New York, NY • Type: Colored Dull Finish Photograph • Postmark: Not Used • Value Index: C

The *AMERICAN FARMER* was constructed in the vast war-built shipyard at Hog Island, PA and was not completed in time for World War I service. She was launched as the *OUROC* and was one of seven steamers owned by the American Merchant Line. These vessels were slightly larger than the American Scantic ships, having a 7,430 gross tonnage (as rebuilt). They were rebuilt to accommodate only 80 passengers and, because the reconstruction occurred before the Scantic ships were rebuilt, their passenger facilities were somewhat less elegant. The five American Merchant Line ships running between New York City and London, England were 448 feet long and had a beam of 58 feet. They were highly popular ships and could made 16 knots. During World War II the ship was renamed *VILLE DE LIEGE* and was torpedoed and sunk in April 1941.

S. S. AMERICAN FARMER

Publisher: American Merchant Lines • Manufacturer: The Albertype Company, Brooklyn, NY • Type: Black-White Artist Conception • Postmark: Not Used • Value Index: E

A TYPICAL STEAMER OF THE AMERICAN EXPORT LINES

Publisher: American Export Lines Export SS Corporation • Manufacturer: Not Indicated • Type: Black-White Dull Finish Photograph • Postmark: Not Used • Value Index: C

The World War I great shipbuilding program was begun too late and the program did leave the United States with a surplus of deep-sea tonnage. Dozens of new overseas ship lines were formed, each was allocated war-built cargo ships. One of the ship lines that became a success was the Export SS Corporation, which linked the United States with Mediterranean ports. Its start-up fleet included a number of Hog Island cargo ships carrying 12 passengers in each ship. This new line began a naming system using ship names beginning with "EX..." and so this particular vessel was named *EXTAVIA*. From the start of their operations the company concluded that having passengers was good business and the passenger portion of the operation slowly prospered. The *EXTAVIA* measured 5,083 gross tons, 390 feet long, and had a beam of 54 feet. The steamer was built in 1919 in the same class as the ships of the American Scantic and American Merchant Lines.

Publisher: United American Lines, Inc. • Manufacturer: Not Indicated • Type: Colored Dull Finish Artist Conception • Postmark: Not Used • Value Index: E

The *RELIANCE* and *RESOLUTE*, in 1914, were part of the Hamburg American Line. Their original names were *JOHANN HEINRICH BURCHARD* and *WILLIAM O'SWALD*. These ships were smaller versions of the giant *IMPERATOR-VATERLAND-BISMARK* class of ships. Each ship measured 19,802 gross tons, had a length of 618 feet, a beam of 72 feet, and three smokestacks. Holland was neutral in the war and the Royal Holland Lloyd Line was able to buy the unfinished liners from the Hamburg American Line in 1916, completed in 1920, and named *LIMBURGIA* and *BRABANTIA*. After brief use the ships were sold to the United American (Harriman) Line for trans-Atlantic service. Renamed again, the twins became the *RELIANCE* and *RESOLUTE*. After being transferred the owner soon discovered that because of Prohibition, liquor could not be offered to passengers. The ships were transferred to Panamanian registry. In 1926 W. Averill Harriman, abandoned his shipping career and the line was sold to the Hamburg American Line. and the ships returned to the German flag. The *RESOLUTE* was sold to Italy in 1935, to become a troopship for Mussolini's ill-fated invasion of Ethiopia and was scrapped in 1940. The *RESOLUTE*, renamed *LOMBARDIA*, was bombed and sunk in Naples, Italy in 1943.

U. S. ARMY HOSPITAL SHIP "ST. MIHIEL"
ARRIVES AT PORT OF EMBARKATION
CHARLESTON, S. C.

Photo by U. S. Army Signal Corps

Publisher: Southern Bell Telephone and Telegraph Company • Manufacturer: Not Indicated • Type: Black-White Dull
Finish Photograph • Postmark: Not Used • Value Index: E

U. S. Army Hospital Ship "Emily H. M. Weder"
Arrives at Port of Embarkation
Charleston, S. C.

Photo by U. S. Army Signal Corps

Publisher: Southern Bell Telephone and Telegraph Company • Manufacturer: Not Indicated • Type: Black-White Dull
Finish Photograph • Postmark: Not Used • Value Index: E

Almost identical in basic dimensions to the seven American Merchant Line Hog Islanders previously described were two other steamers built in 1920 at the Hog Island, PA yard. They were the *CHATEAU THIERRY* and the *ST. MIHIEL*, both completed as troopships and they retained that status through the remainder of their lives, except for short periods of operation as hospital ships. The *ST. MIHIEL* shown in this illustration was able to carry 1,247 troops. Service began in November 1920, running from New York City to Cristobal in the Canal Zone. For the next three years the *ST. MIHIEL* operated in the Atlantic Ocean. After 1923 the Army assigned this steamer to supply the Panama Canal operations and then to move into the Pacific area.

In 1940 the *ST. MIHIEL* was shifted to the Alaskan supply route. Later the ship was redesigned to take 509 bed patients and conversion was accomplished by the Bethlehem Steel Company at their Boston, MA shipyard. The rebuilt steamer in its first mercy voyage during 1944 sailed to Oran, North Africa. In the next several years the *ST. MIHIEL* operated out of Charleston, SC. After a series of voyages to and from England the hospital ship ran aground near Bermuda. A full load of patients had to be transferred to the Army hospital ship *JOHN J. MEANY*. The *ST. MIHIEL* was repaired at Charleston, SC and was sent to the Pacific Ocean. In 1945 the old steamer was decommissioned at Los Angeles, CA and scrapped some years later.

The World War I shipbuilding effort produced more ships for America's deep-sea passenger fleet than any other program in the nation's history. Two major ship types were built from the keel up as troop carriers. They were considerably larger than the Hog Islanders rebuilt as passenger ships such as the *SCANPENN* or the *AMERICAN FARMER* classes. The larger of the two troopship types came to be known as the "535" class because their overall length was 535 feet. The smaller type was called the "502" class as that number was their length. The two types of ships were initially christened with the nicknames of various states. The ship illustrated on the opposite page began life in 1920 as the *PANHANDLE STATE* (nickname for Oklahoma). The ship's dimensions were 10,533 gross tonnage, length 502 feet, and a beam of 62 feet.

None of these troopships were completed in time for service in World War I. Many of the ships were purchased by the Dollar Line and given names of various presidents. This became the *PRESIDENT MONROE*. The two classes of ships had goal-post masts that resembled the goal posts on a football field. The cargo booms were worked from these structures. Three goal-post mast structures can be seen in the photograph.

In 1922 Captain Robert Dollar, founder of the Dollar Line, began an around-the-world passenger-cargo service. In the late 1920s the MONROE was rebuilt with the altered superstructure to increase the passenger capacity. Prior to World War II the company built a new ship which it planned to name *PRESIDENT MONROE* and this steamer was rechristened *PRESIDENT BUCHANAN*. In 1943 a second reconstruction produced the outline shown in the photograph and the ship was renamed *EMILY H.M. WEDER* to honor a nurse who lost her life in the war. After VJ Day the Army used the ship to bring home military troops and dependents. This career lasted until 1953 when the vessel was laid up and sold for scrap.

The *CABO DE BUENA ESPERANZA* was one of the "535"-type steamships, built as a troopship for World War I, but not finished in time to serve in the war. This liner was built in 1921 by New York SB Company, Camden, NJ. The ship was originally named the *HOOSIER STATE*. All ships in this class measured 14,187 gross tons, 535 feet long, and a beam of 72 feet. With turbine propulsion, the *HOOSIER STATE* could reach a speed of 17 knots. This vessel with one other "535" survived because of a strange quirk of fate. With many other ships of the class, the *HOOSIER STATE* was acquired by the Dollar Line in 1922 and renamed the *PRESI-DENT LINCOLN*. The Dollar Line ran the ship between San Francisco, CA and the Far East, a route for which the vessel was ideal because there was space for 480,600 cubic feet of cargo. Passenger accommodations were limited to approximately 300 persons in First and 500 persons in Third Class.

Bad management after the death of Captain Robert Dollar resulted in the line entering into bankruptcy. In 1940 the steamer was sold to Ybarra & Company of Seville, Spain. At first the name *MARIA DEL CARMEN* was assigned to the ex-American troopship.

Publisher: Ibarra Cia.,SA Linea Mediterraneo-Brasil-Plata • Manufacturer: Seix Y. Barral, Barcelona, Spain • Type: Colored Dull Finish Artist Conception • Postmark: Not Used • Value Index: C

Publisher: Ibarra Cia.,SA Linea Sud-America • Manufacturer: Seix Y. Barral, Barcelona • Postmark: Not Used • Value Index: C

The ship was rebuilt to offer First Class space to 824 persons and Third Class transportation to 835 persons on the Spain to South America run. For an unknown reason, the name was changed to *CABO DE BUENA ESPERANZA*. Good fortune continued to be with the vessel and all during World War II this craft steamed back and forth across the South Atlantic Ocean, all lights ablaze.

The upper illustration was issued by Ybarra & Company. It shows the ship's comedor (dining saloon) which had been originally designed for only 300 persons. There must have been three sittings per meal when the ship sailed with a full number of passengers. This liner was scrapped in 1958 and is illustrated below as depicted by a Spanish artist, showing the Ybarra & Company distinctive double-XX markings on her black single smokestack and steaming out to sea. Notice that the goal post type masts remain, although reduced in size by artistic license.

Munargo

THE S.S. "MUNARGO"
OPERATED IN NEW YORK – NASSAU – CUBA PASSENGER SERVICE

MUNSON STEAMSHIP LINES
67 WALL STREET
NEW YORK

After World War I, one of the honored names in American shipping was the Munson Line. Its route was from East Coast ports of the United States to the east coast of South America. This company had built up a reputation of good service and was given the best available war-built ships. In 1921 the company began service with a custom-built little liner for short runs in the Caribbean. Their traditional naming system was to have ships names beginning with "Mun..." as in *MUNARGO*.

Built by New York SB Corporation, Camden, NJ, the *MUNARGO* measured 6,336 gross tons, a length of 413 feet, and a beam of 57 feet. The turbine propulsion plant had 5,800 horsepower and the single propeller provided a top speed of 17 knots. Unfortunately, as the Economic Depression came the Munson Line began to falter in its operations. The *MUNARGO* was sold to the United Fruit Company in 1938, retaining the same name. The War Department purchased the steamer in 1941 and rebuilt the vessel to carry 1,113 troops. An initial proposal was to rename the ship the *ARTHUR MURRAY*. When the Navy took over the vessel the name became the *USS MUNARGO*. Later the ship was converted to a hospital ship, the vessel and *THISTLE*. After more years of service the old craft was scrapped.

Publisher: Munson Steamship Company • Manufacturer: Not Indicated • Type: Sepia Dull Finish Photograph • Postmark: Not Used • Value Index: E

The *PACE* is shown here under Italian ownership, although the steamer began life in 1921 as an American liner. This vessel was first named *CUBA*. With only 2,479 gross tons, the little liner had a length of 325 feet and a beam of 47 feet. Built for the Peninsular & Occidental SS Company the *CUBA* could reach 16 knots with triple expansion, 3,600 horsepower engines. The first 20 years of the ship's life were uneventful. In February 1942 the *CUBA* was taken over for war duty and rebuilt to carry 596 troops and 32,015 cubic feet of cargo. Again the ship's military duty saw little excitement except for one bent propeller requiring brief drydocking. After the war the ship was sold to Italy for operation as a Mediterranean cruise ship the Ignazio Messina Company, Genoa, Italy. A new, wider, and thicker smokestack changed the silhouette completely. Dormitory cabins were installed in place of the cargo holds. An 11-day cruise, priced from $115 up, went from Genoa, Italy to Barcelona, Spain with many stops. The ship was eventually scrapped in the early 1960s.

Publisher: Ignazio Messina & Cie-Genes • Manufacturer: Edizioni, Genova, Italy • Type: Black-White Artist Conception • Postmark: Not Used • Value Index: D

This liner rated with British gross tonnage might have been as high as 20,000 tons, however, the United States tonnage was only 13,712.

The *PAN AMERICA*, as shown in the illustration, began life as the *PALMETTO STATE*, one of the famous "535"s built by the Bethlehem SB Corporation Yard, Sparrows Point, MD. The ship was a fine passenger ship and a large cargo carrier. The steamer was assigned by the Shipping Board to the Munson Line for express service to the east coast of South America. On the first northbound voyage, the *PAN AMERICA* brought home 56,000 bags of coffee as part of 4,400 tons of cargo. The ship's dimensions and speed were similar

Publisher: Munson Steamship Line • Manufacturer: Not Indicated • Type: Sepia Dull Finish Photograph • Postmark: Not Used • Value Index: E

to the other "535" vessels. During World War II, the U.S.Navy renamed this liner *HUNTER LIGGETT* and the ship was given to the Coast Guard for operation. The ship earned four battle stars. Some of the actions in which the *HUNTER LIGGETT* gave support were the capture and defense of Guadalcanal, the consolidation of the Solomon Islands, and the Treasury-Bougainville operation. The war-weary craft was laid up in 1946 and scrapped eight years later.

The noted German marine artist Willie Stower, famous for his painting of the sinking *TITANIC*, painted this view of the *PRESIDENT ADAMS*, originally the *CENTENNIAL STATE*. It was completed while the "502" type steamer was in the New York City to London, England service of United States Lines between 1921 and 1923. As first commissioned this steamer had 10,496 gross tons, a length of 502 feet, and a beam of 62 feet. In 1940 the Dollar Line, then known as American President Lines, was building several new passenger ships and planned to name one of them after President Adams. The steamer in this illustration was renamed *PRESIDENT GRANT*. The ship was rebuilt to carry 1,776 troops and the ship began a war career for the Army leaving San Francisco, CA for Manilla,

Publisher: United State Lines • Manufacturer: Not Indicated • Type: Colored Dull Finish Painting • Postmark: Not Used • Value Index: C

Philippines in November 1941 with continuous service in the Pacific Ocean. The *PRESIDENT GRANT*'s last sailing from San Francisco, CA was on February 2, 1944 and disaster came at a point only 70 miles off Milne Bay, Philippines. The troopship grounded on Uluma Reef and was lost. Fortunately all persons aboard were saved.

On Board
U. S. Government
S. S. "President Polk"

UNITED STATES LINES
Operators for U. S. Shipping Board

Publisher: United States Lines • Manufacturer: Not Indicated • Type: Colored Dull Finish Painting • Postmark: Not Used • Value Index: E

Another fine Postcard illustration painted by an important marine artist; Worden Wood's initials, W.W., are in the lower right corner. The painting shows one of the "502"s, the *PRESIDENT POLK*, originally named *GRANITE STATE*. The ship was built at Camden, NJ by the New York SB Corporation. The painting shows this steamer when she operated briefly in the trans-Atlantic service for U.S. Lines. The Dollar Line ran the ship on the Pacific during the period between World Wars I and II. In 1940, this classic-styled liner was renamed *PRESIDENT TAYLOR*. The company always reserved the names of the more famous presidents for their newer or larger steamers. The *TAYLOR* had one of the shortest careers of all World War troopships, as the ship was grounded February 14, 1942 on a coral reef at Caton Island. Abandoned, the ship was later destroyed by a Japanese air attack. When she was in service for the United States Lines a number of Postcards were issued for the *PRESIDENT POLK*. In each caption on the back of the Postcards the ship's overall length was given as 522 feet instead of 502 feet. length. The United States Line tried to establish the nickname "522" instead of "502" but they never succeeded.

Publisher: Dollar Steamship Lines • Manufacturer: Not Indicated • Type: Colored Dull Finish Painting • Postmark: Not Used • Value Index: E

The *PRESIDENT JEFFERSON*, illustrated with an unnamed artist's conception, was the first of all the "535"s. This ship's first name was *WENATCHEE*. Renamed *PRESIDENT JEFFERSON* the steamer was given to American Mail Line for a route between Pacific Northwest ports and the Orient. This company became associated with the Dollar Line and was later absorbed by that much larger firm. The company was popularly called the Dollar Steamship Lines and its homeport was San Francisco, CA. The *PRESIDENT JEFFERSON*'s dimensions were the same as all other "535"s.

Unfortunately, in the 1930s, the Dollar Line had financial problems. When the second generation of Dollar Line family took over the line it went bankrupt and a United States government-owned company was created to operate their ships. The company assumed the name of American President Lines. World War II increased the demand for ships and the U.S. Government operation turned out to be very profitable. After World War II, the firm, which has been converted into a private company, has become one of the most successful in the Merchant Marine. The *PRESIDENT JEFFERSON* became the transport *HENRY T. ALLEN* during World War II and was finally sold for scrap on March 26, 1948.

This photograph shows the *ALASKA*, built in 1923 by Todd Dry Dock & Construction Company, Tacoma, WA, a vessel notable as one of America's earliest experiments with turbo-electric propulsion. This power system was later chosen for the great French Line record breaker *NORMANDIE*. The *ALASKA* measured 4,511 gross tons, a length of 365 feet, and a beam of 49 feet. The ship's 15-knot speed and 4,780 mile cruising radius was ideal for the long run to Alaska both in peace and in war.

Publisher: Not Indicated • Manufacturer: Not Indicated • Type: Black-White Glossy Photograph • Postmark: Not Used • Value Index: E

Rebuilt early in 1942 for troopship service, the steamer's capacity was raised to 355 men. All during the war the vessel ran on charter to the War Shipping Administration, averaging one round trip per month. The *ALASKA* was known for regularity of service. When the war ended she was one of only seven Alaska Line passenger ships returned by the United States government to private use. The Alaskan Line did its best to win back its business, but competition from commercial air services became stronger each year.

This illustration shows the *ALASKA* slowly approaching a pier in Alaskan waters. The ship's cargo booms are shown as having been unlimbered and are ready to work. After a decade of postwar service, the *ALASKA* was sold in 1955, renamed *MAZATLAN*, and was scrapped within a short time.

This vessel was the "A" ship in the Merchants & Miners Line known as the "Alphabet Fleet" of coastwise passenger ships. Each of their steamers were named after a different county in Maryland, Virginia, and Massachusetts, with one ship's name starting with each letter of the alphabet, or nearly each letter. When this liner was new in 1923, the fleet had names beginning with two-thirds of the letters of the alphabet. The *ALLEGHANY* ran between Boston, MA, Norfolk, VA, and Newport News, VA, with occasional calls at Philadelphia, PA, Baltimore, MD, and Miami, FL.

Publisher: Steamship Historical Scoiety of America • Manufacturer: Not Indicated • Type: Black-White Glossy Photograph • Postmark: Not Used • Value Index: E

The *ALLEGHANY* was built by the Federal Shipyard at Kearny, NJ, and was a ship of 6,950 gross tonnage, slightly larger than the *ALASKA*. The *ALLEGHANY* was 368 feet long, a beam of 52 feet, and a speed of 13 knots. The *ALLEGHANY* was renamed *AMERICAN SEAFARER* during World War II and used as a training ship. The ship's long life ended in 1949 in a scrapyard.

Publisher: United States Lines • Manufacturer: Printed in USA • Type: Colored Dull Finish Photograph • Postmark: Not Used • Value Index: F

The *PRESIDENT ROOSEVELT* was launched at the New York Ship Yard in Camden, NJ, and initially christened *PENINSULA STATE*. Later the U.S. Shipping Board changed the name to *PRESIDENT PIERCE* and then to *PRESIDENT ROOSEVELT*. In World War II, the *PRESIDENT ROOSEVELT* was renamed *JOSEPH T. DICKMAN* for troop carrying service. Leading a charmed life, the vessel sailed continuously on both Atlantic and Pacific Oceans. The ship was decommissioned in early 1946; the sturdy survivor lasted until scrapped in 1948.

One of the best know episodes in the life of the *PRESIDENT ROOSEVELT* occurred in the mid-Atlantic during January 1926. Captain George Fried went to the rescue of a British cargo ship, the *ANTINOE* in a fierce storm. Captain Fried's battle with the elements lasted four days and he used every technique that he knew. Unfortunately, he lost five of his own ship's lifeboats and two members of his heroic crew during the rescue effort. In the last hours of the rescue fog set in over the scene. The *PRESIDENT ROOSEVELT* disappeared in the fog for a few minutes to the horror of the seamen aboard the sinking *ANTINOE*. When the *PRESIDENT ROOSEVELT* returned to sight someone on the *ANTINOE* hoisted a flag signal saying: "Please Don't Leave Us." In reply Captain Fried ordered this signal flag sent up his mast: "I Will Not Abandon You." All hands on the freighter were saved.

The *CATSKILL*, shown in this illustration, was always something of an ugly duckling. Built in 1923, the vessel was designed for cargo service by the Catskill Evening Line on the Hudson River. The ship had only 652 gross tonnage, was 186 feet in length, and 40 feet wide. An upper deck was added when the ship was sold for passenger-cargo service. While serving on the Long Island Sound Ferry run, the ship had her single smokestack placed slightly aft of center, always giving her an out-of-balance appearance. She did not have any masts; however, there were two large poles for flags at the bow and stern to provide her with a bit of style.

THE STEEL STEAMER "CATSKILL" CARRYING PASSENGERS AND AUTOMOBILES BETWEEN EASTERN LONG ISLAND POINTS AND NEW LONDON, CONN.

Publisher: United States Maritime Service • Manufacturer: Not Indicated • Type: Blue Ink Dull Finish Photograph • Postmark: Not Used • Value Index: D

A model of this vessel is on display at the Ships of the Sea Museum, Savannah, GA. During World War II, this beautiful ship was listed in official records as a "Floating Hotel." The *AMERICAN NAVIGATOR* was used to train thousands of men to become ship engineers and navigators in the Merchant Marine. A pair of gun tubs are shown replacing the main mast aft. Note the life rafts and the machine gun emplacement aft of the bridge. The ship was 401 feet in length, a 52-foot beam, and measured 6,500 gross tons.

While operating for the Savannah Line, the

★ U. S. M. S. T. S. AMERICAN NAVIGATOR ★

Publisher: United States Maritime Service • Manufacturer: Not Indicated • Type: Blue Ink Dull Finish Photograph • Postmark: Not Used • Value Index: D

ship ran between New York City and Savannah, GA. Deck plans show there were ten deluxe cabins each with twin beds and a private bath. Every cabin had hot and cold running water, a 12-inch electric fan, and a vacuum bottle for drinking water. Public rooms included a music room, writing room, and sun lounge. This ship was scrapped in 1948.

The British liner shown in this illustration was built in 1923. Between 1923 and 1938 the one-stacked steamship was the *MONGOLIA*, of the Peninsular and Oriental Line, which linked Great Britain with India and Australia. Then the 16-knot speed *MONGOLIA* was chartered to the New Zealand Shipping Company and renamed *RIMUTAKA* for use on the London, England to Wellington, New Zealand run. After long use in World War II, the ship was renamed *EUROPA* for the Incres Line. This illustration shows the *EUROPA* operating between Havre, France and New York City. Cruising was growing in popularity, particularly to the Caribbean

Publisher: Incres Compania De Navegacion • Manufacturer: Not Indicated, Printed in USA • Type: Black-White Dull Finish Photograph • Postmark: Not Used • Value Index: E

and the steamer was renamed *NASSAU*. In 1961 a new owner rebuilt the *NASSAU* for use from Southern California to Mexico's west coast with a new name *ACAPULCO*.

Mexico was not a signatory to the international safety rules for ships. This ship did not have the reciprocity available with the American authorities. The United States Coast Guard was obliged to order drastic safety improvements to be made. The owner could not afford these improvements and the liner's career ended. In late 1964, the *ACAPULCO* was towed across the Pacific and scrapped.

This ship was built in 1923 and served under the house flag of the Inter-Island Steam Navigation Company of Honolulu, HI. Named *HALEAKALA*, this little liner was built in Chester, Pa and had 3,679 gross tons, a length of 345 feet, and a beam of 46 feet. A crew of 73 was required for operation of the ship, with home port at Honolulu, HI. Note that the long bow is without a well deck forward when compared to the *ALASKA*. The lower promenade deck is actually an extension of the long bow, continuing an old-style feature. Also, note the smoke stack, larger and wider

Publisher: Steamship Historical Society of America • Manufacturer: Not Indicated • Type: Black-White Glossy Photograph • Postmark: Not Used • Value Index: E

than the smokestacks of other ships in the same period of time, a decidedly modern feature. Passengers shown in this photograph are disembarking at the lower promenade into life boats lowered from the after davits. The ship is at anchor off shore, obviously at a port which did not have sufficient depth to allow a large ship to come any closer into shore. Or, perhaps there was no pier often the situation for a ship in the Hawaiian islands.

HUDSON RIVER DAY LINE STEAMER
ALEXANDER HAMILTON

Publisher: Hudson River Day Line • Manufacturer: The Albertype Company, Brooklyn, NY • Type: Colored Dull Finish Photograph • Postmark: Not Used • Value Index: F

The 2,367 gross ton *ALEXANDER HAMILTON* was put in service in May 1924, and ran continuously until 1972 when she was towed to South Street Seaport Museum, New York City. The Seaport could not support the ship and the deterioration of the equipment and the ship was obvious as time passed. Eventually, a restaurant owner acquired the *ALEXANDER HAMILTON* and towed the famous steamer away to his location in New Jersey. The ship sank in a storm at a Navy pier in New Jersey and the loss of this ship was mourned by many people. D. C. Ringwald's book, **HUDSON RIVER DAY LINE** published in 1965, has many photographs of this stately steamer and the text describing the ship is quite complete.

The *ALEXANDER HAMILTON* remained in service longer than any other Day Line vessel. She came to be known to millions of New Yorkers. The steamer's dimensions were 349 feet in overall length, 77 feet wide, and 8 feet draft. She was built by the Sparrows Point Shipbuilding Corporation, MD. and cost $852,000. Paintings by Herbert W. Faulkner showing scenes in the life of Alexander Hamilton were used as decorations throughout the steamer's interior.

STANDARD FRUIT STRS-AMAPALA & ATLANTIDA ③

Publisher: Standard Fruit Line • Manufacturer: Lumiton Photoprint, New York, NY • Type: Colored Dull Finish
Photograph • Postmark: Not Legible • Value Index: E

This Postcard was issued by the Standard Fruit Company to publicize their ``Swift, Oil-Burning Steamers *AMAPALA* and *ATLANTIDA*." These twin liners "Maintain A High Standard Of Comfort, Courtesy and Service." They offered 13-day cruises sailing every Saturday to Santiago, Cuba, Kingston, Jamaica, and La Ceiba, Honduras. New Orleans, LA was their home port.

The *AMAPALA* was built by Swan, Hunter and Wigham Richardson, Ltd., Newcastle, England, in 1924. With 4,148 gross tons, the ship was 350 feet in length, and a beam of 50 feet. Triple expansion engines with a single screw gave the *AMAPALA* a speed of 15 knots. The Standard Fruit Company was generally known as the Vaccaro Line named after the family that had founded it at the turn of the century. The principal cargo was bananas; however, four passenger ships also did a lively cruise business and were popular among travelers. They were all painted white with a red waterline. Sad to say, the *AMAPALA* was torpedoed off the mouth of the Mississippi River in May 1942. The *ALANTIDA* survived the war and was not scrapped until 1960.

The S.S. *BOSTON*, a new Eastern Steamship Lines flagship running between Boston, MA and New York City had the maiden trip on June 4, 1924. A sister was named *NEW YORK*. These ships were remarkably different from all other overnight vessels. They looked larger than they were and this illusion added a sad postscript to their careers.

In September 1942, both were part of the famous ``Skimming Dish'' trans-Atlantic convoy, whose code name was RB-1. Both ships were torpedoed on the way over and the German radio proudly announced sinking two troopships of the *QUEEN MARY* class. What

S. S. "BOSTON" ON EASTERN S. S. LINES, INCORPORATED.

Publisher: Eastern Steamship Lines, Card No. 118879 • Manufacturer: Tichnor Quality Views • Type: Colored Dull Finish Painting • Postmark: Not Used • Value Index: F

a tribute to their design. In reality they were only 385 feet long, a beam of 72 feet, and 4,989 gross tons compared to the *QUEEN MARY*'s 80,774 gross tons. Both were built by the Bethlehem Steel yard at Sparrows Point, MD and required a crew of 186 people. They had 2,680 horsepower and could make 19 knots.

The RB-1 convoy was made up of small coastal liners whose hulls were considerably more narrow than their overhanging superstructures which lead to the naming of the convoy after a skimming dish, wider at the top edge than the bottom. None of the ships should have attempted to cross the ocean. England was in desperate need of ships and all available ships were sent.

This steamer was named the *DISTRICT OF COLUMBIA* and together with the *NORTHLAND* and the *SOUTHLAND*, maintained a daily service between Norfolk, VA and Washington, DC under the house flag of the Norfolk & Washington SB Co. All three were handsome overnight boats, fast, well-maintained, and offering a service that is missed in these days of massive traffic jams and crowded highways. The *DISTRICT OF COLUMBIA* was built in 1924 at Wilmington, DE. With 2,128 gross tons, this steamer was 297 feet long and 51 feet wide. The line was absorbed into

Publisher: Norfolk and Washington Steamboat Company • Manufacturer: Beals Litho Tone, Des Moines, IA • Type: Black-White Dull Photograph • Postmark: Not Used • Value Index: E

the Old Bay Line (Founded in 1840) and when the Old Bay Line closed out in 1962 that ended the longest-lived ship line in American history.

The *DISTRICT OF COLUMBIA* was renamed *PROVINCETOWN* and moved to Massachusetts Bay. The ship's last active service was in 1963. In 1969, at Baltimore, MD. and with the name *DISTRICT OF COLUMBIA* back on the pilot house, the vessel suffered a serious fire. Finally in 1973, the *DISTRICT OF COLUMBIA* sank in the harbor. The venerable hulk gradually broke up and disappeared.

Although the Old Dominion Line's *GEORGE WASHINGTON* was approximately one-half the size of the smallest trans-Atlantic liners of the era, she served as a regular Atlantic passenger ship. She was Hull No. 276 of the Newport News SB & DD Company, Newport News, VA. The 5,184 gross ton ship was launched August 20, 1924, and completed on November 16, 1924.The Economic Depression caused the Old Dominion Line to charter the *GEORGE WASHINGTON* to other ship lines.This photograph was taken while the ship was on a run, at Ketchikan, AL. After America's entrance into World War II, the sistership *GEORGE WASHINGTON* and the *ROBERT E. LEE* were taken by the Army for troopship service.

Publisher: General Steamship Corporation, Seattle, WA • Manufacturer: Not Indicated • Type: Black-White Glossy Photograph • Postmark: Not Used • Value Index: D

A humorous incident occurred at Bermuda when military authorities tried to force 8,000 troops aboard the ship, insisting they were following War Department instructions. The Master of the *GEORGE WASHINGTON* knew that his ship had been converted to carry only 778 people. His objections went unheeded. While the troops were beginning to board the little liner, someone shouted and pointed to the outline of a much larger steamer approaching; also named the *GEORGE WASHINGTON*. The veteran ship was sold to Hong Kong ship breakers in 1955.

The *GREATER DETROIT*, shown here, and the *GREATER BUFFALO* were the largest sidewheel steamers ever constructed excepting the *GREAT EASTERN* built as Brunel's mammoth experiment of 1859. The two ships were built in 1924 at Lorain, OH, as slightly enlarged versions of the *CITY OF DETROIT III*. These sisterships dimensions: a 7,739 gross tonnage, length of 550 feet, beam of 100 feet, 12,000 horsepower, speed 21 miles per hour (the company chose not to use knots). They could accommodate 2,127 passengers in 625 staterooms. There were 26 "Parlors with Bath," 130 staterooms with toilets, and space to carry 125 automobiles.

Publisher: National Railway News Company,Inc., Card No. 119853 • Manufacturer: Tichnor Quality Views • Type: Colored Dull Finish Painting • Postmark: Not Used • Value Index: F

The *GREATER BUFFALO* was converted for use as an aircraft carrier to train World War II flyers and was located on the Great Lakes. Renamed *SABLE*, the big steamer was so drastically altered in the conversion process that when peace came reconversion was not possible and the vessel was scrapped. The *GREATER BUFFALO*'s fame, however, has been perpetuated through election to the *National Maritime Hall of Fame*. After World War II, the *GREATER DETROIT* remained in service This historic steamer was scrapped in 1950.

The Clyde-Mallory Line had four steamers built in 1925 and 1926. The first two were christened *CHEROKEE* and *SEMINOLE*. Two other sisters were named *MOHAWK* and *ALGONQUIN*. These ships were built to run between New York City and Miami, FL, The steamers measured 5,896 gross tons, a length of 402 feet and had a beam of 55 feet. With 4,200 horsepower, each had a speed of 15 knots and required 110 crew members. The illustration shown here must have been issued in mid-1935 or later as the ill-fated *MOHAWK* is not mentioned. The *CHEROKEE* was first, launched February 10, 1925, as Hull No. 274 of the Newport

Publisher: Clyde-Mallory Lines, Card No. E-4150, Manufacturer: Not Indicated • Type: Sepia Dull Finish Painting • Postmark: Not Used • Value Index: E

News SB & DD Co., Newport News, VA. The *CHEROKEE* was lost on June 15, 1942 after being torpedoed by a German submarine east of Boston, MA with a loss of twenty people. The *SEMINOLE* was launched April 14, 1925 and delivered on August 19, 1925. She was taken over for war service early in 1942. The vessel was hurried into troopship duties with a quick rebuilding that enabled her to carry 500 soldiers. Although not designed for ocean service, the little *SEMINOLE* made many trips across the Atlantic in 1942 and early 1943. The ship served until October 1945 then laid up and sold for scrap.

"American Flag Ships to Puerto Rico and the Dominican Republic" is the description on the back of this Postcard. The company listed its name as the "New York and Porto Rico S.S. Co," using the old spelling. The *COAMO* was built by the *Newport News* Shipyard. Mrs. Franklin D. Mooney officiated at the christening on July 22, 1925 as the wife of the owner of the Atlantic Gulf and West Indies combine. The *COAMO* was a little larger than the *CHEROKEE* and *SEMINOLE*, with 7,000 gross tonnage, a length 429 feet, and a beam of 60 feet. The steamer had turbine propulsion with a top speed of slightly more than 16 knots.

The ship's last Master was Captain Nels Helgesen. Very

STEAMSHIP COAMO ~ PORTO RICO LINE

Publisher: New York and Porto Rico SS Company, New York, NY • Lumitone Photoprint, New York, NY • Type: Colored Dull Finish Painting • Postmark: Not Used • Value Index: E

little is known about the *COAMO*'s last voyage. The ship was ordered to cross the Atlantic Ocean and pick up troops in North Africa to be taken to England. The *COAMO* accomplished the trip and then headed for home in a convoy. For reasons never explained, the British Admiralty instructed the *COAMO* to leave the convoy and continue alone. The ship was never heard from again. Extensive research has gone into the mysterious disappearance of the ship with all hands aboard.

The *NOBSKA* was built in 1925 at Bath Iron Works, Bath, ME for the New Bedford, Martha's Vineyard and Nantucket Steamboat Line. This ferry service had grown to be one of the busiest and most important water routes in New England. In 1925 the operators embarked on the largest new ship project ever attempted in that area. They planned to build three new large-size sisterships and added a plan for a fourth ship to exceed these ships in size. The *NOBSKA* is one of the three new sisters. Renamed *NANTUCKET*, the 1,082-gross-ton vessel served for many years with success. Currently, and with

Publisher: Not Indicated • Manufacturer: Tichnor Quality Views • Type: Colored Dull Finish Photograph • Postmark: Not Used • Value Index: E

the original name back on the stern, this steamer is being restored by a group known as "Friends of NOBSKA, Inc.", a nonprofit preservation society. The *NOBSKA*'s dimensions were 210 feet long, 50 feet wide, and 1,000 horsepower. The ship cost $300,000 in 1925. Artist *W. G. Muller*, speaking aboard the *NOBSKA* on September 24, 1989, set the steamer's future when he said:

"*NOBSKA* has become the last surviving example of the classic, plumb-bow'd, tall-stacked American coastal steamer. NOBSKA's own history is rich and important, and so we must not just save this boat; we must bring her back to vibrant life. Looking at NOBSKA now, we see a proud and stately shell containing a great steam engine-the perfect foundation."

The third and fourth new Clyde-Mallory Line steamers, *ALGONQUIN* and *MOHAWK* had much more exciting lives than did the earlier ships. The *ALGONQUIN* collided with and sank another liner, the *FORT VICTORIA*. The accident occurred near Ambrose Lightship in a dense fog. Fortunately, no life was lost on either ship. On July 3, 1940, the *ALGONQUIN* burned at Pier 34 on the Hudson River, New York City, and siank into the mud directly over the Manhattan end of the Holland Tunnel. One report said that 50 firemen were overcome in the three alarm blaze. Radio and news accounts high-

Publisher: Not Indicated * Manufacturer: Southern Bell Telephone and Telegraph Company,Inc. Type: Black-White Dull Finish Photograph * Postmark: Not Used * Value Index: E

lighted fears that the ship might have damaged the Holland Tunnel; however, there was no damage to the tunnel and the ship was raised, repaired, and put back into service. At the end of the war the ship was converted to bring home military dependents and war brides. The vessel was scrapped a few years later.

Publisher: Delta Queen Steamboat Company, Fas Foto, Inc. • Manufacturer: Plastick By Colour, Boston, MA • Type: Colored Glossy Photograph • Postmark: Cincinnati, OH 1982 • Value Index: F

Publisher: Frank O. Braynard • Stevenson Printers, Inc. Glen Cove, NY • Type: Sepia Dull Finish Drawing • Postmark: Not Used • Value Index: F

The illustration shows this grand old lady of America's inland waterways and highlights the steamboat's magnificent stern wheel. The *DELTA QUEEN*, revered by many as the personification of a magnificent Mississippi River sternwheeler, is really much more. The steamer was built on the River Clyde, Scotland, between 1924 and 1926, with paddle wheel, shafts and cranks made in Germany. She was disassembled and shipped via the Panama Canal to California for overnight service on the Sacramento River. A sistership was named *DELTA KING*. Both vessels did war service in San Francisco Bay.

The 1,837-ton *DELTA QUEEN* was purchased by the Greene Line in 1948 for service on the Mississippi River. Captain Fred Way, Jr., was responsible for the purchase and the towing of the *DELTA QUEEN* from San Francisco, CA, through the Panama Canal, and up to New Orleans, LA. The *DELTA QUEEN* has been in continuous operation on the Mississippi and the Ohio rivers. The historic craft continues to operate despite noncompliance with the Coast Guard regulations. The owners plan to rebuild the ship to eliminate the need for a special exemption. The vessel has become an historic landmark. Each year the *DELTA QUEEN* and the newer and larger *MISSISSIPPI QUEEN* race each other from New Orleans to either Cincinnati, OH or St. Louis, MO.

The last of the new ships built in 1926 for the Merchants & Miners Company, the *DORCHESTER* had many luxuries. The ship included French-style telephones in every cabin, felt-lined windows which cut out the rattle often heard aboard a ship, hot and cold running water, an electric fan in every cabin, a berth light, and a bottle for storing water. Seven of the steamer's cabins had a private bathtub, while 16 had showers. The *DORCHESTER* was built at Newport News, VA and measured 5,649 gross tons, 368 feet long, and 52 feet in beam. The reciprocating engines drove the new steamer at 13 knots. The *DORCHESTER* is remembered because of a World War II incident. Daniel A. Poling wrote a column for the Philadelphia Record newspaper in which he said:

"Men have come to have great affection for the ships on which they sail. There was an intimacy between them and the decks they trod that was to me an inspiration always and a reassurance when the storms came. But if ever a ship had a soul and lives on forever, that ship is the *DORCHESTER*, once the pride of the Chesapeake. Converted into a troop transport the *DORCHESTER* sailed the North Atlantic in the days when enemy submarines took their heaviest toll. It was early on the morning of Feb. 3, 1943, in iceberg waters off Greenland that she came to her heroic death. Ten minutes before one o'clock a torpedo struck home, stopped her engines and blew out her heart. Scores of Army personnel and crewmen died below her decks and other hundreds, under the Northern Lights, succumbed in the freezing waters. Only three lifeboats ever got away and at dawn in these many were found frozen at the oars. Of the 904 total personnel on the *DORCHESTER* 687 were lost. When her prow rose high and her careening decks slid under, the great ship carried many heroes with her, and, of these, four have become immortal. They were chaplains — two Protestants, a Catholic and a Jew —whose citations tell us that they moved among the personnel, quieting panic, giving reassurance, and that finally they took off their own life belts and gave them to enlisted men. Then when they had done all they could, and each of his own faith, they prayed together. In that last fated moment they were seen on the deck, but never again."

Theodore Ferris was one of America's finest naval architects and marine engineers. Among many of his smaller steamers was the *CARACAS* built in 1927. The ship was part of the Red ``D'' Line, an almost forgotten ship line operating ships on the Philadelphia, PA to Venezuela route since 1838.

The letter "D" came from the owner the Dallett Family of Philadelphia, PA. The company's formal name was Atlantic & Caribbean Steam Navigation Company. The *CARACAS* was a three-island-type steamer, with a forecastle, central superstructure, and poop with well decks forward and aft.

RED "D" LINE
S. S. "CARACAS"
NEW YORK TO PORTO RICO, CURAÇAO & VENEZUELA

Publisher: Red "D" Line • Manufacturer: Not Indicated • Type: Gray Tone Dull Finish Photograph • Postmark: Not Used • Value Index: D

The *CARACAS* had a 336-foot length, 51 foot beam, 3,500 horsepower, and 13 knots top speed. In 1937 the Red "D" Line was absorbed by the *Grace Line* and the *CARACAS* was sold to the *Alaska Line* and renamed *DENALI*. The government rebuilt the steamer for war service. After the war the *DENALI* was rebuilt for cruising. In 1954 the ship was sold to Peninsular & Occidental SS Company who renamed the ship *CUBA*. Business problems caused the transfer to the Liberian flag, renamed as *SOUTHERN CROSS*, and finally to Belgian scrappers.

The steamer shown in this illustration was built in 1927, the Clyde-Mallory Line*'s IROQUOIS* was described as "The Largest, Finest, and Fastest passenger liner ever built for American coastwise service." When the Japanese bombed Pearl Harbor, HI this liner was there in the dress of a hospital ship and named *SOLACE*. Two important architectural features were introduced by Theodore Ferris in this ship. One innovation was the bulbous bow, a rounded steel protrusion under the water at the stem of the vessel which was designed to reduce vacuum and increase speed. This innovative feature was put on public display unintentionally when the *IRO-QUOIS* ran aground in 1936. The *BREMEN* built in 1929 has usually been credited with introducing the bulbous bow. The second innovation was the extension of the superstructure over four-fifths of the vessel's length, a feature now seen on all modern cruise liners. The steamer's dimensions were 6,209 gross tons, 394 feet in length, and 62 feet in beam.

CLYDE-MALLORY LINERS, S.S. IROQUOIS AND S.S. SHAWNEE

Publisher:Clyde-Mallory Lines, Card No. 64435 • Manufacturer: Tichnor Bros., Inc. 1472 Broadway, New York, NY • Type: Colored Dull Finish Painting • Postmark: Quebec, Canada, August 3, 1938 • Value Index: E

The *MALOLO* built in 1927 for Matson Line was in service between the American West Coast and Hawaii. The ship was designed by William Francis Gibbs. The construction of the *MALOLO* was said to have been responsible for bankrupting the Wm. Cramp & Sons Ship and Engine Company of Philadelphia, PA because Gibbs was so demanding and forceful in his design ideas. The success of his design became apparent when the ship was struck by a freighter. Gibbs had installed extensive compartments and watertight doors that could be closed from the bridge. The *MALOLO* remain afloat and kept an even keel despite a hole as

Publisher: Home Lines • Manufacturer: G. Schenone, Genoa, Italy • Type: Colored Dull Finish Photograph • Postmark: Not Used • Value Index: F

large as the hole that sank the *TITANIC*. In 1937 the *MALOLO* was renamed *MATSONIA*. When World War II came she served as a troopship. In 1947 the liner was acquired by *Home Lines* and renamed *ATLANTIC*. The ship was 582 feet long and had a beam of 83 feet. The twin screws permitted this vessel to reach a top speed of 21 knots.

In 1955 the National Hellenic American Line renamed the steamer *QUEEN FREDERICA*. The ship was used briefly as a floating prop for a motion picture film being prepared on the raising of the *TITANIC*. In 1978 a fire ended the ship's career.

The *DIXIE*'s keel was laid at the Federal Shipyard, Kearny, NJ on January 31, 1927. The 8,100-gross-ton ship was launched July 29, 1927, made a trial trip on December 10, and entered service on January 28, 1928, from New York City. This $2,400,000 steamship was built for the Southern Pacific Steamship Lines, however, everyone knew it as the Morgan Line. The ship was 445 feet in length, had a beam 60 feet, 8,000 horsepower, a speed of 16 knots, and a crew of 114 people. This steamship was more luxurious than many coastal ships, and was able to carry 420,000 cubic feet of cargo. The

SOUTHERN PACIFIC STEAMSHIP LINES—"MORGAN LINE"

NEW YORK—NEW ORLEANS   NEW STEAMSHIP DIXIE

Publisher: Southern Pacific Steamship Lines • Manufacturer: Not Indicated • Type: Colored Dull Finish Painting • Postmark: Not Used • Value Index: E

ship's four Babcock and Wilcox watertube boilers were an advanced design with a steam pressure of 350 pounds-per-square-inch. The ship was driven by a single propeller. On January 21, 1941, the *DIXIE* was purchased by the United States Navy and renamed *ALCOR* for war service as a repair ship and a destroyer tender. After the war, the name reverted to *DIXIE* and later sold for scrap.

Two sisterships built in 1927 for the Eastern Steamship Company were important ships for several reasons. The *YARMOUTH*, older by three months, lasted beyond the half-century mark. The *EVANGELINE* was a victim in one of the country's worst maritime fires. In their later lives each ship was renamed *YARMOUTH CASTLE,* causing confusion in maritime historical studies.

Both ships came from Wm. Cramp & Son Ship & Engine Company, Philadelphia, PA. They were among the last of the ships built by the Cramp Company. Each was designed by Theodore Ferris and measured 5,043 gross tons, length 378 feet, beam 55 feet, 7,500 horsepower, speed of 16 knots, and a crew of 141 people. They were built for the overnight run between Boston, MA and Yarmouth, Nova Scotia. The *YARMOUTH*'s maiden voyage from Boston began on July 9, 1927. The *EVANGELINE* was completed in September 1927.

The *YARMOUTH* was first to enter World War II. The *EVANGELINE* was taken over by the War Department 30 days after the attack on Pearl Harbor, HI and operated under charter in the Caribbean. Both ships were rebuilt as troopships in 1942.

In February 1946 the two ships were returned to Eastern Steamship Company, a company that was strong enough to survive the war and wanted to return to peacetime operation. In 1965 the Chadade SS Company acquired the *EVAN-*

S.S. Yarmouth, Yarmouth, N.S.

Publisher: W.R.Rozee, Yarmouth, Nova Scotia * Manufacturer: Novelty Manufacturing Company,Ltd., Montreal, Canada * Type: Colored Dull Finish Painting * Postmark: Not Used * Value Index: E

S/S Evangelene

Publisher: Steamship Historial Society of America, United States Signal Corps Port of Embarkation, New York * Manufacturer: Not Indicated * Type: Black-White Glossy Photograph * Postmark: Not Used * Value Index: D

GELINE and the name became *YARMOUTH CASTLE*. On November 13, 1965, the much neglected ship, with lifeboats that could not be launched and inadequate safety equipment, caught fire off Great Stirrup Key, Bahamas and 90 passengers died.

The final years of the *YARMOUTH* were extraordinary because of the many names given to the ship. In 1954 the original name was changed to *YARMOUTH CASTLE*, and in the same year the owners changed the name again to *QUEEN OF NASSAU*. In 1957 the ship became the *YARMOUTH CASTLE* again and renamed *YARMOUTH* in the same year. When the ship was sold in 1967 the name was changed to *SAN ANDROS*. Sold the following year, the name became the *ELIZABETH A*. The scrapper's torch was applied in 1977.

Albert F. Haas was the naval architect for the New England Steamship Company's three ferries, built between 1923 and 1928, for travel between Martha's Vineyard, MA and Nantucket, RI. The *ISLANDER* was completed first and was renamed *MARTHA'S VINEYARD*. Then the *NOBSKA* was completed, renamed *NANTUCKET*, and last, the *NEW BEDFORD* was constructed. All three had the same dimensions. Although the *NEW BEDFORD* measured only 1,117 gross tons, this sturdy little Bethlehem-built ferry succeeded in crossing the Atlantic during World War II as part of the "Skimming Dish" Convoy.

STR. NEW BEDFORD AT WHARF, OAK BLUFFS, MASS.   123564

Publisher: Not Indicated • Manufacturer: C.T. American Art • Type: Colored Dull Finish Photograph • Postmark: Not Used • Value Index: F

The fact that the *NEW BEDFORD* completed the round trip was quite a feat for a ferry. The steamer was launched May 5, 1928 and given to the owners only 14 days later.

A 1928 report about the new vessel stated: "It is of interest to note that the owner continues to use coal as fuel." Although the two-deck superstructure was constructed of steel, the two top deck houses were made of wood. "On the upper deck of the vessel there is a wooden house for the president's room and for officers' accommodations. The wooden pilot house is equipped with the usual navigating outfit and allows maximum visibility."

This ferry was the largest and finest ship built for service to Martha's Vineyard, MA and Nantucket, RI. The ship was also a veteran of World War II service near the Normandy beachhead. The steamer was named *NAUSHON* when built in 1929 by the Bethlehem SB Corporation at the Quincy, MA yard. The vessel measured 1,978 gross tons, 240 feet long, and 45 feet wide. During the initial use of the vessel the *NAUSHON* had a smokestack that was too low and passengers complained of soot on the after deck and the stack was made taller.

During World War II a wounded soldier was taken aboard the

Steamer Naushon

New Bedford, Marthas Vineyard and Nantucket Steamboat Line. Mass.   66822

Publisher: New Bedford, Marthas Vineyard and Nantucket Steamboat Line, MA • Manufacturer: Tichnor Bros., Boston, MA • Type: Colored Dull Finish Photograph • Postmark: Not used • Value Index: E

NAUSHON unconscious. By coincidence he was from Martha's Vineyard. When he awoke and saw the familiar surroundings he said: "I must be in heaven — on the *NAUSHON*." In 1947 the Meseck Steamboat Company bought the ship and renamed her *JOHN A. MESECK*. In 1968 the old lady was bought by the Marine Engineers Beneficial Association and taken to Norfolk for use as a union training school.

Publisher: Flotta Lauro, Napoli-Genova, Italy • Manufacturer: Di Mauro-Cava, Napoli, Italy • Type: Colored Dull Finish Painting • Postmark: Not used • Value Index: E

Publisher: The Interstate Company • Manufacturer: The Albertype Company, Brooklyn, NY • Type: Colored Dull Finish Photograph • Postmark: Not Used • Value Index: E

You may not believe that the two ships shown in the illustrations on the opposite page started their lives as identical sisterships. The upper illustration is the *SURRIENTO*, originally the *SANTA MARIA*, built in 1928. The illustration below is the *SANTA CLARA*, built in 1929 and rebuilt in 1936. A third sister was the *SANTA BARBARA*. The three ships were ordered by Grace Line, the *SANTA MARIA* and *SANTA BARBARA* in England and the *SANTA CLARA* at New York Ship, Camden, NJ. All of the ships were slightly less than 9,000 gross tons, 486 feet long, and 64 feet wide. The English-built pair were motor ships. The Camden-built vessel used turbo electric propulsion, a newly innovative power system at the time. All three ships were twin screw vessels and could reach 16 knots.

They were one-class ships with space for 150 passengers. It was noted in Marine Engineering and Shipping Age magazine for June 1928 that the British twins had two smokestacks, "Although, of course, they are by no means essential." This comment did not mention the fact that the public had made its likes and dislikes known. Motor ships without smokestacks were not popular. Another trend that was noticed and commented upon:

"One of the features of the ships is that the number of cabins with bathrooms adjoining represents a far bigger proportion than is usually to be found in passenger vessels. It would almost seem as if some shipowners, like hotel proprietors, are coming to the conclusion that what the public now demands is sleeping accommodation with adjoining bathrooms, and the additional expenditure is, no doubt, well warranted."

This thinking, slow and hesitant as it may sound, was far in advance of most other shipping people in 1928. Another 1928 comment indicates how slow some naval architects were to look ahead:

"It is difficult to provide novelties in passenger liners in these days. But one interesting feature is to be noted. Each cabin, for instance, has a special device in the roof, with the object of indicating immediately in the wheelhouse should a fire occur, and of locating it without any delay."

What type of thinking would call such an absolutely essential fire prevention device a "novelty."

During World War II the *SANTA MARIA* served as the troopship *BARNETT*. After the war the ship's reconstruction for the Achille Lauro Line was drastic. The two old motorship stacks were replaced by a large, streamlined dummy funnel. Both prewar masts were eliminated and a single tripod mast was erected above the new pilot house. The superstructure and old cargo holds were completely rebuilt to offer space for 187 passengers in First Class and 868 passengers in Tourist Class. Air conditioning, unheard of in 1928, was provided throughout the ship. The *SANTA CLARA* was sunk during the invasion of Normandy, without any loss of life. The *SANTA BARBARA*, renamed *SUSAN B. ANTHONY*, was lost in 1943.

S. S. Pennsylvania   Panama Pacific Line

Publisher: The Interstate Company • Manufacturer: The Albertype Company, Brooklyn, NY • Type: Black-White Dull Finish Photograph • Postmark: Not Used • Value Index: E

October 1, 1927, was a great day for Philip A.S. Franklin, President of the International Mercantile Marine (IMM) and his daughter, Mrs. Roland Palmego. She sponsored the new Panama Pacific Line turbo-electric liner *CALIFORNIA*. J.P. Morgan's combine was starting to build a fleet of new American flag passenger ships. Newport News SB & DD Company had the contract for the first and second ships and everyone hoped there would be a third ship. The first new liner was the *CALIFORNIA*, The second was named *VIRGINIA*, and the third became the *PENNSYLVANIA*.

(Continued on next page)

The upper illustration shows the *PENNSYLVANIA* as initially built. The trio was taken back by the government because the IMM failed to pay the annual installments on their cost of construction. As Panama Pacific Line ships they ran, for a decade, between New York City and San Francisco, CA. During this time the seamen had a corrupt union which had signed an agreement giving up overtime for the workers. A young bosun's mate, Joe Curran, aboard the *CALIFORNIA* began a sitdown strike and one of the results of the strike was the formation of a powerful new maritime union calling itself the National Maritime Union. The IMM was tired of dealing with union problems and gave up its three new American steamers. Then President Franklin D. Roosevelt stepped into the action. With his flair for the dramatic he named the trio of ships his "Good Neighbor Fleet" and assigned them to the Moore McCormack Lines to run to the east coast of South America. They were renamed *ARGENTINA* (ex-*PENNSYLVANIA*), *BRAZIL* (ex-*VIRGINIA*), and *URUGUAY* (ex-*CALIFORNIA).*

Below is an artist's conception of the *ARGENTINA* showing how the original dummy stack aft was replaced by a larger single funnel. All three ships survived the war, although the *URUGUAY* had a close call. On February 12, 1943, this liner, still operating under the Moore McCormack name, was in a collision near Bermuda with the Navy tanker *SALOMONIE*. For years very few knew that some 30 *URUGUAY* men were killed in this accident. During the war each of the three ships was rebuilt to carry nearly 5,000 men. Roland Charles in his book **TROOPSHIPS OF WORLD WAR II**, said that only a few other ships carried more men and women to and from the war fronts. All three were restored for another decade of service.

Publisher: Moore-McCormack Lines • Manufacturer: Henry H. Baumann, 254-6 W. 31st Street, New York, NY • Type: Colored Dull Finish Painting • Postmark: Not Used • Value Index: D

This illustration shows the *CONTESSA* steaming out of Havana Harbor. No liner had more interesting war experiences than this 5,512-gross-ton beauty. One especially rugged adventure began in May 1942, when the *CONTESSA* was scheduled to carry gasoline and ammunition up the uncharted Sebou River in North Africa to supply American troops assigned to seize an enemy airport. Unfortunately, the heavily laden ship ran aground halfway up the river. Captain William John prayed that high tide would release him and watched anxiously as the ship slowly floated free. To his horror, however, he saw the swirling waters begin to turn him around in the narrow river, his bow facing downstream. Not to be beaten in his efforts he steamed the remainder of the trip in reverse. The Vaccaro Line steamer, sailing under the Honduran Flag, was 381 feet long and 53 feet wide. The ship had been built in 1930 by Barclay, Curle & Company, Glasgow, Scotland. The ship was rebuilt after their war service.

VACCARO LINE. NEW STEAMER CONTESSA

Publisher: Standard Fruit and Steamship Company, Card No. 2A420 • Manufacturer: Thomas Dunne Company, New Orleans, LA • Type: Sepia Toned Dull Finish Photograph • Postmark: Not Used • Value Index: D

The *CONTESSA* served until 1959 when the steamer was towed to Rotterdam and renamed *LEEUWARDEN*. She may be in use today.

The *ORIENTE*, built in 1930 by the Newport News SB & DD Company had everything that the sister-ship *MORRO CASTLE*, did not have. The steamer was famous for being at sea every day of the year making the weekly 2,400-mile round trip from New York City to Havana, Cuba. The dimensions were: length 508 feet and width 71 feet. The ship's second smokestack was a dummy. The *ORIENTE*'s turbo-electric power drove the ship's two 16-foot diameter propellers at 144 revolutions per minute, producing a speed of 20 knots. Originally, the liner was known as a Ward Line steamer, but after the burning of the *MORRO CASTLE*, the Ward name was changed to Cuba Mail Line. In 1936 the twin stacks of the ORIENTE were painted all black to avoid looking too much like the *MORRO CASTLE*.

TURBO ELECTRIC LINER ORIENTE

Publisher: New York and Cuba Mail SS Company • Manufacturer: Lumitone Photoprint, New York, NY • Type: Colored Dull Finish Photograph • Postmark: Not Used • Value Index: E

In 1941 the ship was purchased by the United States Army and renamed *THOMAS H. BARRY* to accommodate 3,609 troops. The old ship, with many sad associations to the tragic *MORRO CASTLE*, was scrapped in 1957.

The *EXCALIBUR* and her three sisterships built in 1930 at New York SB Co., Camden, NJ are among the most beautiful little liners afloat. They were owned by the American Export Lines and traveled from New York City on 45-day cruises to the Mediterranean. They measured 9,359 gross tonnage, had a length of 451 feet, a beam of 66 feet, and a speed of 16 knots. At a time when many designers adopted the somewhat ugly cruiser stern, these ships had old-style counter sterns. Also, while many lines were experimenting with square smokestacks, low and flat-topped stacks, or no stacks, these steamers were given a single beautifully raked funnel, perfectly proportioned in height, width, and length. Their masts were the correct height, bows tall and clean cut, and superstructure pleasing to the eye. These ships were designed by George Sharp.

In the upper illustration of the *EXCALIBUR* there are two groupings of five tall slit windows just above the black hull line under the middle and the third lifeboats. These windows faced out from two large communal verandas which offered semiprivate deck space to four veranda staterooms. The illustration below shows a cabin on the *EXO-CHORDA*, longest-lived of the four sisterships was the

Publisher: American Export Lines • Manufacturer: The Albertype Company, Brooklyn, NY • Type: Black-White Dull Finish Photograph • Postmark: Not Used • Value Index: E

Veranda Stateroom

Publisher: American Export Lines • Manufacturer: Harry H. Baumann, 254-6 W. 31st Street, New York, NY • Type: Colored Dull Finish Photograph • Postmark: Not Used • Value Index: D

only one of the quartet to survive the war, and then was sold to Turkey. The steamer was renamed *TARSUS* and served in the Mediterranean. The sad ending for the ship was described in a message written to the author on June 3, 1961:

> "I saw the old *EXOCHORDA* in bad shape in Turkey . . . She had just come out of the yard after a refit, and was lying at anchor. Two big tankers got in collision. . . . and the burning oil drifted onto the *TARSUS* and burned her out, killing a lot of customs people on board. She is lying at anchor in the Bosporus with a bad list, waiting for the lawsuit to be settled."

This illustration shows another coastal liner that served as a trans-Atlantic passenger ship. The *BORINQUEN* was launched on September 24, 1930 as flagship of the New York & Porto Rico Line (old spelling). This 7,114-gross-ton steamer had four other names: *PUERTO RICO* in 1949, *AROSA STAR* in 1954, *BAHAMA STAR* in 1959, and *LA JANELLE* in 1970. Perhaps the ship's most dramatic moment was when the *YARMOUTH CASTLE* was on fire and Captain Carl Netherland-Brown rescued 378 survivors. Captain Carl told the author a striking detail of this episode. The burning ship's Master, who shall be nameless here, was in the first

Publisher: Eastern Steamship Corporation, Miami, FL • Manufacturer: Dexter Press,Inc., West Nyack, NY Type: Colored Glossy Photograph • Postmark: Not Used • Value Index: E

lifeboat to leave the stricken vessel. Captain Carl refused to take the Master aboard his ship and sent him back to his own ship. Years later Captain Carl remembered the *BAHAMA STAR* with these words: "She was a wonderful old ship, which we all loved In 1968, when the new international Safety Standards came into effect, we so regretted that it would be totally uneconomic to upgrade the 37-year-old *STAR*. She simply had to go."

The Dollar Line's flagship *PRESIDENT HOOVER* was built in 1931 by the Newport News SB & DD Company. The ship was the largest passenger ship built in America when she was new. The ship's turbo-electric power plant helped convince the French Line to use this type of engine in the superliner *NORMANDIE*. This liner cost $8,000,000 to build and, with a sistership named *PRESIDENT COOLIDGE*, the two ships gave America a leading position on the Pacific Ocean. The dimensions of the liners were: 21,936 gross tonnage, 654 foot length, 81 foot beam, and capable of making 22 knots. Their interiors were spacious and beautiful. On December

Publisher: Dollar Steamship Lines • Manufacturer: Not Indicated, Printed in USA • Type: Colored Dull Finish Painting • Postmark: Not Used • Value Index: E

11, 1937 this liner ran aground near Formosa, west of Hoishoto Island. All aboard were saved, however, the ship was lost and immediately scrapped. A friend loaned the author a scrapbook of photographs maintained by one of the ship's officers covering the delivery voyage to the disaster. In the scrapbook are some horrendous wreck photographs. The photographs were taken from ashore and show how the pounding of huge waves cracked and broke up the ship's hull within only two days. One photograph of the steamer in a head-on view shows a single wave completely enveloping the big liner, curling in a 200-foot high arc over the top of the masts.

Publisher: Eastern Steamship Lines, Inc. and Harry McKinlay, Yarmouth, Nova Scotia, Card No. 135633 •
Manufacturer: Tichnor Quality Views • Type: Colored Dull Finish Photgraph • Postmark: Not Used • Value Index: F

Publisher: Chandris Lines • Manufacturer: Not Indicated, Printed in England • Type: Colored Glossy Photograph • Postmark: New York, NY, 27 May 1942 • Value Index: F

The sisterships *ACADIA* (upper photograph) and *SAINT JOHN*. These ships were the 15th and 16th passenger ships built by Newport News SB & DD Company to the design of naval architect Theodore Ferris. These vessels were the last ships built for the Eastern Steamship Lines because World War II ended operations for this company.

The two ships ran between New York City and Boston, MA during the winter and on various cruise routes in the summer. The *ACADIA*'s last peacetime charter was to the Alcoa SS Company in 1941 to cruise the Caribbean. This

(Continued on the next page)

ship was chartered to the United States Army one year before Pearl Harbor; she was rebuilt as a troopship. After we entered World War II the ship was reconstructed as a hospital transport. Three trips were made in this service from North Africa to New York City and then the steamer was disarmed and became a full hospital ship with room for 738 patients. The *ACADIA* was the first United States vessel to be rebuilt in this manner. The only accident in the *ACADIA*'s war career was striking a submerged object at Oran, North Africa. In 1955 the young liner was sold to a Swiss company and went to the ship breakers. Built in 1932 and originally called the *MONTEREY* this long-lived liner continues to operate at this writing. The *MONTEREY* was the second of the Matson Trio to be completed by Bethlehem at their Quincy, MA yard. Two ships, the *MONTEREY* and the *MARIPOSA* maintained the Australian-New Zealand run The *MONTEREY* began with a length of 632 feet. In 1957 the length was increased to 642 feet when the ship was modified and renamed *MATSONIA*. This change was done by adding a *NORMANDIE*-style bow to the steamer. The 18,017 gross tonnage increased to approximately 25,000 gross tons when measured under foreign rules. As a Greek-owned ship in 1970 the liner was renamed *BRITANIS*, meaning "British Girl". During World War II this steamer, with an 18,000-mile radius, was an ideal troopship. The most dramatic moment came on November 6, 1942, when the *MONTEREY* was close to the Grace Line's *SANTA ELENA* near Philippeville, Algeria. The *SANTA ELENA* was hit by an aerial-launched German torpedo and started to sink. Although several enemy bombers were in the area, the *MONTEREY* stopped and saved most of the survivors. Hunter Wood, painter in residence at the United States Merchant Marine Academy captured the scene with his oil painting. To the right in the scene is the *SANTA ELENA* sinking in the water.

Publisher: Chandris Lines • Manufacturer: Not Indicated, Printed in England • Type: Colored Glossy Painting • Postmark: Not Used • Value Index: F

As built in 1932, the *LURLINE* had 18,021 gross tonnage. When purchased in 1963 by the Chandris Lines and renamed *ELLENIS* (meaning Greek Girl) the measurement increased to 24,351 gross tons. In World War II the *LURLINE* served in the Pacific Ocean, except for one voyage to Marseilles, France. This gallant ship's destination points is a list of major naval engagements: Guadalcanal, Espiritu Santo, Milne Bay, Ulithi, and others. The *LURLINE*, whose name was not changed for war service, returned to San Francisco, CA on May 8, 1946. Then the Matson Line made an amazing error. The Federal Government offered to rebuild the *MARIPOSA*, *MONTEREY*, and *LURLINE* at government expense before returning them to the ship line, or to give the company the money so that the line could have the rebuilding done. The Matson Line chose the latter and unanticipated inflation and poor cost estimates caused the Matson Line to spend all the money on one ship, the *LURLINE*. The two others were laid-up, and continuing embarrassment to the Matson Line management. Eventually they were rebuilt.

A single-ship operation was resumed in April 1948. The LURLINE was sold to Chandris in 1963 and the name was changed to ELLENIS. After 15 years of service as an immigrant ship to Australia and cruising out of England the *ELLENIS* was scrapped in the mid-1980s.

This painting is shows how marine artists actually led naval architects in ship exterior design concepts. There were two problems with the smokestacks in this painting of the United States Lines' steamship *MANHATTAN*. The artist knew the real stacks were not sufficiently wide and thick. The artist painted them the way he thought they should be. The French Line was the only ship line that recognized this situation. In 1931 they planned a superliner and commissioned several marine artists to draw the ship they would like to build. The work of one artist was used in the final exterior design of the *NORMANDIE*. The shortness of the twin stacks was an effort to make

Publisher: United States Lines • Manufacturer: Not Indicated, Printed in USA • Type: Colored Dull Finish Painting • Postmark: Not Used • Value Index: E

the ship look streamlined, (the naval architect forgot the soot problem) and the stacks had to be doubled in height. The painting was made from the original blueprints.

When World War II began, the liner made a few voyages to the Mediterranean and then went into intercoastal service. In January 1941 the MANHATTAN was grounded near Florida and required $2,000,000 in repairs. When the ship was taken over for war use the vessel was renamed *WAKEFIELD*. The *WAKEFIELD* served until May 1946. The great liner was unwanted for nearly 20 years and was scrapped in 1964.

The *MARIPOSA* sailed from the Bethlehem Steel Company's Quincy, MA yard early in January 1932. The new ship had a measurement of 18,017 gross tons in contrast to the 3,158 gross tons of the company's original ship with the same name built in 1883. The dimensions were 631 feet in length, 79 feet wide, and the ship could make 20 knots. The ship entered the South Pacific run.

When World War II began the three new Matson liners were taken into military service. The Matson Line was unable to pay for the restoration of the luxury liner when war ended. Home Lines bought her in 1953. From 1955 until 1963 the liner had the new name *HOMERIC*. The *HOMERIC* suf-

THE SS MARIPOSA, 632 FEET LONG; 79 FEET BREADTH; GROSS TONNAGE 19,000; SPEED 20½ KNOTS

Publisher: Matson Line, Card No. 26632N • Manufacturer: E.C. Kropp Company, Milwaukee, WI • Type: Colored Dull Finish Painting • Postmark: Not Used • Value Index: E

fered a serious pier fire at New York City in mid-1973. Damage to the interior was so severe that the ship had to be scrapped.

Two little liners built in 1932 for the Columbian Line were named the *HAITI* and the *COLOMBIA*. The Newport News SB & DD Company had the contract for their construction as Hulls No. 347 and 348. They were 404 feet long, 57 feet wide, a crew of 93, 5,200 gross tons, and the builders anticipated that they would be able to make 17 knots with a single screw drive. The ships operated between New York City, Haiti, Jamaica, Panama, and Colombia in 1933, marking the first time the Colombian Line had passenger vessels. The rates were set at $10 a day, everything included, and for a time business boomed. The Ward Line bought the *COLOMBIA* in 1938, renamed the *ship MEXICO*, and as-

Steamships MEXICO and MONTEREY

Publisher: New York and Cuba Mail SS Company • Manufacturer: Lumitone Photoprint, New York, NY • Type: Color Dull Finish Photograph • Postmark: Not Used • Value Index: E

signed the liner to their Cuba-Mexico service. The *HAITI* was also sold to the Ward Line that year, renamed *PUERTO RICO*, then again renamed *MONTEREY* to run with the *MEXICO*. Both ships were taken over early in 1942 for war duties. Their 7,000-mile cruising radius and high speed made them valuable as troop carriers until decommissioned mid-1946. The relatively new sisterships were sold to Turkey, the *MEXICO* renamed the *ISTANBUL* and the *MONTEREY* the *ADANA*. Both ships were rebuilt by Todd Shipyards, Brooklyn, NY. The ships operated from Istanbul, Turkey for 30 years of successful service.

Frederick Sands, Grace Line Vice President had three ships named *SANTA PAULA* at the same time. They also had two ships named *SANTA ROSA*. In 1958, when the Grace Line was building a new *SANTA ROSA* and about to christen the new hull at Newport News, VA, the company's old ship of the same name, shown in this illustration, was in operation. She was ordered to the shipyard where the new ship was to be launched. As a result there were two *SANTA ROSAs* afloat . The situation with the three *SANTA PAULAs* is more complicated. The Grace Line laid up the original

S. S. Santa Rosa   Grace Line

Publisher: The Interstate Company • Manufacturer: The Albertype Company, Brooklyn, NY • Type: Colored Dull Finish Painting • Postmark: Not Used • Value Index: E

SANTA PAULA just before their new ship was christened. However, the old ship still had the name *SANTA PAULA* on the stern. Then the old *SANTA ROSA* was renamed *SANTA PAULA* to prevent confusion among travelers, as this vessel would operate with the new *SANTA ROSA* until the new *SANTA PAULA* arrived. The result was three ships named *SANTA PAULA*.

With a white diamond on a red stripe around the middle of their tall single smokestacks, the ships of the United Fruit Company were easy to identify. Their fleet included more than 20 ships, with the largest carrying a significant number of cruise passengers. Six liners were built under the Jones-White Act of 1928, a law that offered construction subsidies for vessels built with a potential of being able to serve as Naval Auxiliaries in war. When World War II arrived all of the ships proved their worth and survived five years of strenuous war duties.

S.S. TALAMANCA, one of six sister ships of the GREAT WHITE FLEET—UNITED FRUIT COMPANY

Publisher: Not Indicated (Probably United Fruit Company) • Manufacturer: Harry H. Baumann, 216 W. 18th Street, New York, NY • Type: Colored Dull Finish Photograph • Postmark: Not Used • Value Index: E

The first ship of this new fleet was the TALAMANCA, shown in this illustration in a artist's conception. This ship served as a United States Navy Storeship in World War II without being given a new name. All six ships had the same dimensions: length 448 feet and width 60 feet. Each had a 6,982 gross tonnage measurement. Each ship could carry 113 passengers in First Class and 245,800 cubic feet of cargo, usually bananas. The TALAMANCA, PETEN, and CHIRIQUI were built by Newport News SB & DD Company, while the ANTIGUA, QUIRIGUA, and VERAGUA were constructed by Bethlehem Steel Company at Quincy, MA. The TALAMANCA and the four other ships led comparatively quiet lives. All were sold to foreign owners and given new names. They were scrapped in the late 1960s.

Built at Wilmington, DE in 1933, this rather ugly but highly practical steamship is not as large as indicated at first impression. The ship is named the DEL-MAR-VA, the meaning of which can be guessed without difficulty, as the car and truck ferry linked Delaware, Maryland, and Virginia. The vessel was owned by the Virginia Ferry Company of

Publisher: Not Indicated • Manufacturer: Rowe Distributing, Norfolk, VA • Type Colored Glossy Oversize Photograph • Postmark: Norfolk, VA, October 22, 1962 • Value Index: F

Cape Charles, VA and measured 1,496 gross tons, a length of 249 feet, and a breadth of 95 feet. The vessel was a double ender and designed to carry both cars and trucks on the lower deck. A careful look far aft   on the top or Boat Deck, you can see a large open steering wheel, a return to the days when Greek or Egyptian sailing craft were steered at this point with a long steering oar. The steering oar was on the right side of the ship leaving the left side free for docking. This configuration was the origin of the two words Port and Starboard. Port, or left, was the side always next to the pier or dock. The other side was the steering board side, which if said repeatedly and quickly was eventually cut down to Starboard side.

This illustration shows a cleverly faked photograph of the *SANTA ELENA* going from the Grace Line pier down the Hudson River, NY, passing lower Manhattan, and heading for the sea. The ship portion of the photograph was carefully cut out and superimposed on the downtown New York City skyline. A careful look shows the dome between the two funnels which could be rolled back to open the ship's beautiful First Class dining saloon to the sky.

When the *SANTA ELENA* was being constructed at the Federal Shipyard in Kearny, NJ, pictures of the launching for the first two sisters were published in the

S. S. Santa Elena

Publisher: Interstate Company • Manufacturer: The Albertype Company, Brooklyn, NY • Type: Colored Dull Finish Photograph • Postmark: Not Used • Value Index: E

rotogravure sections of many newspapers showing all four new Grace Line ships. The tonnage and dimensions of this ship are similar to those of the *SANTA ROSA*. The *SANTA ELENA* was in private service when Pearl Harbor, HI was bombed. By January 23, 1942, this little liner had been taken over and outfitted for the United States Army Transport Service. The *SANTA ELENA* name was not changed as a troopship. Voyaging across the Atlantic several times the ship was near Philippeville, Algeria on November 6, 1943, when sunk by a German torpedo plane. The crew and troops were rescued by the Matson liner *MONTEREY*.

The *SANTA LUCIA* was the third of the four passenger ships designed by Gibbs & Cox for the Grace Line and built at Federal Shipyard, Kearny, NJ in 1932 and 1933. All were extraordinary vessels, sleek and very luxurious. This illustration shows the *SANTA LUCIA* in World War II, after the Navy had taken the ship from the Army. Although the vessel had steamed across the Pacific for the Army under the Grace Line name, the Navy renamed the steamer the *LEEDSTOWN*.

In this photograph the ship is at New York City. A forward gun tub is clearly visible. Another feature is the world's first Sampan smokestack,

S/S Santa Lucia

Publisher: Steamship Historical Society of America • United States Army Signal Corps Port of Embarkation, NY • Type: Black-White Glossy Photograph • Postmark: Not Used • Value Index: D

unique to this Grace Line quartet. It was designed, using wind tunnel tests, to be certain that ash and soot from the stack did not descend on the diners on the promenade deck. It was not required for the dummy rear stack. The Sampan design appealed to theship designers and was copied repeatedly on steamships of all types, from tankers to great liners. The *LEEDSTOWN* was torpedoed off Algiers on November 9, 1942 and beached to avoid sinking. The hulk remained there for years and was not salvaged until after the war had ended.

The dimensions of the *WASHINGTON* are: length 705 feet, width 86 feet, and 23,626 gross tonnage. This latter figure reflects the lack of genuine enthusiasm at the United States Lines for their fine steamboats, the *MANHATTAN* and the *WASHINGTON*. When the ships stopped at a foreign port they had to pay port dues based on their rated foreign tonnage, over 30,000 gross tons, which was clearly shown on their papers tacked up in the pilot house. If this rating had been used for public relations on the brochures and deck plans, it would have been apparent that the American ships were larger than the White Star *BRITANNIC and GEORGIC*, or French Line

S. S. WASHINGTON   United States Lines   15
Length, 667 Feet - Breadth, 86 Feet - Gross Tonnage 23,626

Publisher: United States Lines • Manufacturer: A. Mainzer, 118 E. 28th Street, New York, NY • Type: Black-White Glossy Photograph • Postmark: Not Used • Value Index: E

CHAMPLAIN, their principal competitors. Perhaps the worst neglect of all was the fact that the company never restored either of the ships after the war. The *WASHINGTON* was used for a short time as a dormitory ship, then laid up with the *MANHATTAN*. Any foreign line would have restored both ships and used them for many years. The *MANHATTAN* had less than eight years of trans-Atlantic commercial use while the *WASHINGTON* had only seven years. They were scrapped in 1965.

Three small liners (two illustrated on the next page), were built in 1939 by the Bethlehem Steel's Quincy, MA shipyard had long and productive lives. They were the *ANCON, CRISTOBAL,* and *PANAMA* of the Panama Line, a government-owned company linking New York City and New Orleans, LA with the Panama Canal. The three ships were built to the imaginative designs of George Sharp, an American naval architect. The upper illustration shows the *ANCON* and the illustration below shows the *PANAMA* after the ship had been sold to American President Lines in 1957 and renamed *PRESIDENT HOOVER*. Fred J. Hoertz did the painting of the *ANCON*.

These three 10,021-gross-ton ships looked ultra-modern as they went to the scrapyard. They were among the few ships ever built with no sheer rise at the bow and stern. Their smokestack was large enough to make any artist happy and their superstructure was streamlined in a functional way that resisted the passage of time. Each ship carried 216 passengers in First Class, and had a speed of 17 knots.

World War II caused all three ships to be placed into service as troopships. The *ANCON* was given for war service on January 11, 1942 at the Canal Zone and served as an auxiliary amphibious force flagship with the United States Navy during 1943-1946. She was returned to the Panama Line on February 25, 1946. The *CRISTOBAL* was assigned to the Quartermaster General shortly spent the war carrying troops and dependents. The ship returned to the Panama Line on June 14, 1946. The *PANAMA* was in the Army Transport Service on June 13, 1941 and renamed the *JAMES PARKER*, in the West Indies, Pacific Ocean, and North African waters. In early 1946 the ship brought military dependents home and returned to the Panama Line on May 15, 1946.

The *PANAMA* was the first to leave the Panama Line and joined the American President Lines. In 1965 the American President Lines sold the ship to the Chandris Lines. The liner was renamed *REGINA*, spent 13 years under this house flag, and then was laid up at Perma near Piraeus, Greece. In 1988 the ship was scrapped. The *ANCON*, after operating as a cadet training ship for the Maine Maritime Academy under the name *STATE OF MAINE*, was scrapped in 1973 in New Jersey. The *CRISTOBAL* was not scrapped until 1982. Then the ship's massive brass bell, extra-large builder's plate, and a fine model were donated by the Panama R.R. Company to the American Merchant Marine Museum where they have been put on display.

Publisher: Panama Line, Card No. GPO 946638 • Manufacturer: Not Indicated • Type: Colored Dull Finish Painting • Postmark: Not Used • Value Index: E

Publisher: American President Lines • Manufacturer: Not Indicated, Litho in USA • Colored Glossy Painting • Postmark: Not Used • Value Index: E

(See descriptions on the previous page)

This ship was constructed in 1940 by the Bethlehem Sparrows Point, MD shipyard and was originally built for the Delta Line of New Orleans, LA as the *DELBRASIL*, the first of six similar passenger-cargo ships. This steamship made history from the beginning as the first all-welded passenger ship and a pioneer in the use of aluminum furniture and shipboard equipment. After three years of operation, the *DELBRASIL* was taken over by the United States Navy and renamed *GEORGE F. ELLIOTT*, replacing a transport of the same name sunk off Guadalcanal in 1942. As the first of these Delta Line ships were taken over the company ordered three more ships. Two of the second group of three ships had the same names as two of the first group creating considerable confusion among ship historians. The third ship of the first group began life as the *DELTARGENTINO*. The United States Army took this ship in 1941and she became the *J.W. MCANDREW*. These sisterships measured 7,996 gross tons, were 491 feet long, and had a beam of 65 feet. They had 450 pounds of steam pressure-per-square inch. In 1949 the Farrell Line bought them for passenger and cargo service between New York City and South Africa. The *DELBRASIL* became the *AFRICAN ENDEAVOR*, while the *DELARGENTINO* was renamed *AFRICAN ENTERPRISE* which is illustrated in this photograph.

Publisher: Farrell Lines • Manufacturer: Harry H. Baumann, New York, NY • Type: Black-White Dull Finish Photograph • Postmark: Not Used • Value Index: E

The *SEVEN SEAS*, shown in this illustration, began as a large cargo liner christened *MORMACMAIL*, and was launched in 1940 by Sun SB & DD Company, Chester, PA. When almost completed the vessel was given to the United States Navy for an experiment. They had a requirement for aircraft carriers. This vessel was 492 feet long and 69 feet wide, with diesel engines and a speed of more than 16 knots.The ship was renamed *LONG ISLAND* and *Escort Carrier No.1* and became the prototype of the famous CVE class of escort carriers. The conversion was a success and many other C-3 type cargo ships and some oil tankers had the same conversion. Sold after the war to Italian interests, the vessel was converted to carry 1,300 immigrants to Australia, given the odd name of *NELLY*, during 1949 and 1953. Sold again, she became the *SEVEN SEAS* and transformed into a 12,575-gross-ton liner. She operated under the Europe-Canada Line. In 1963 the ship was rebuilt becoming a floating university and was scrapped in 1977.

Publisher: Europe-Canada Line • Manufacturer: Not Indicated • Type: Colored Dull Finish Photograph • Postmark: Not Used • Value Index: D

S.S. "AMERICA" United States Lines Luxury Liner
35,440 Tons, the largest and finest ship ever built in this country   11

Publisher: United States Lines • Manufacturer: Foto Seal Company, New York, NY • Type: Black-White Glossy Photograph • Postmark: Not Used • Value Index: F

The gross tonnage of the *AMERICA*, the largest liner ever built in the United States prior to the *S.S. UNITED STATES*, rose from 26,314 gross tons to 33,532 gross tons, when Walter Jones, public relations director of United States Lines, accepted the author's idea that he should use the ship's British tonnage. This illustration shows a photo of the *AMERICA* entering New York City in 1940. The ship's two smokestacks had been raised 15 feet at the Newport News shipyard following the ship's trials, the streamlined low style allowed too much soot to fall on the after decks. The *AMERICA* was launched on August 31, 1939. The ship was 723 feet long and had a beam of 93 feet. Twin propellers could drive the *AMERICA* at well above the 23-knot contract speed. Because of World War II, the ship made a cruise to the West Indies as a maiden voyage. Shortly after this trip the Navy took possession and renamed the ship *WEST POINT*. During the five years of service the big liner carried 200,000 men outbound and 100,000 home, making 35 overseas voyages. When returned to United States Lines in 1946 the steamer was restored to luxury liner status. In November 1946 the *AMERICA* made an Eastbound Atlantic crossing at an average speed of 24.54 knots. This passage required four days, 22 hours, and 22 minutes between the Ambrose Light and Daunt's Lightship. The ship's life under the American flag coincided with a period of intense union activity and power. In September 1963 a jurisdictional strike began which lasted until the following February. Largely as a result of this strike, the United States Lines sold the ship to the Chandris Line. They renamed the ship *AUSTRALIS*, meaning "Australian Girl." The ship operated until airline competition ended this phase. For a short time the ship was again named *AMERICA*, while a travel agent tried to start a cruise ship service out of New York City. The effort did not succeed.

Chandris Line again purchased the vessel making a large profit in the process. They renamed the steamship *ITALIS*. Various schemes for the ship were proposed, however, the old *ITALIS* was laid up near Piraeus, Greece. In 1989 she broke loose from the anchorage and drifted ashore. At this writing the scrapping operation has begun.

During World War II the American Merchant Marine was expanding its passenger fleet with 27 new liners, built for six ship lines, and the majority were of the C-3 class similar to the *SEVEN SEAS*. Seven were built at Newport News, VA for the American President Lines. They were named after Presidents. The order of their hull numbers was #379 *PRESIDENT JACKSON*, #380 *PRESIDENT MONROE*, #381 *PRESIDENT HAYES*, #382 *PRESIDENT GARFIELD*, #383 *PRESIDENT ADAMS*, #384 *PRESIDENT VAN BUREN*, and, skipping one hull number, #388 *PRESIDENT POLK*. Only the *PRESI-*

Publisher: American President Lines • Manufacturer: Not Indicated • Type: Colored Glossy Painting • Postmark: Not Used • Value Index: E

DENTS POLK and *MONROE* survived the war and were placed on the world circling run. The *PRESIDENT POLK* in the illustration is sailing under the Oakland Bay Bridge. Note the Goal Post Masts, a part of the family inheritance from *Dollar Line* days. The ship was sold in 1965 and renamed *GAUCHO MARTIN FIERRO* and then *MINOTAUROS*. The ship was scrapped in 1970.

This ship began life as the *DELTARGENTINO*, built for *Delta Line* service. This vessel was the second ship Delta had named *DELTARGENTINO*; the first ship was renamed the *J.W. ANDREWS* and then the *AFRICAN ENTER-PRISE*. This new *DELTARGENTINO* was launched at the Bethlehem Steel Sparrows Point, MD shipyard. Before the vessel was completed the hull was taken over by the government and finished as the troopship with the name *MON-ROVIA*. On December 1, 1942 the *MONROVIA* sailed as flagship of Vice Admiral H.K. Howitt for North Africa. On June 30, 1943, General George S. Patton came aboard in preparation for the assault on Sicily. The ship was attacked by a German Stuka dive bomber, but not damaged. Shortly after the attack a high-level strategy meeting was held aboard with Admiral Howitt, General Patton, and

Publisher: The Kimac Company, Guilford, CT • Manufacturer: Not Indicated • Type: Black-White Glossy Photgraph • Postmark: Great Neck, NY, July 23, 1986 • Value Index: D

Admiral Lord Louis Mountbatten. The ship's later war years were spent in the Pacific Ocean. The *MONROVIA* won six battle stars for six actions. In January 1947 the steamer was decommissioned and laid up. This illustration shows the *MONROVIA* in Venice, Italy on a training mission in October 1964, after having been activated again.

U. S. Army Hospital Ship "Wisteria"
Arrives at Port of Embarkation
Charleston, S. C.

Photo by U. S. Army Signal Corps

Publisher: Southern Bell Telephone and Telegraph Company, Inc. • Manufacturer: Not Indicated • Type: Black-White Dull Finish Photograph • Postmark: Not Used • Value Index: E

The Liberty ship program of World War II was a vital factor in winning the war for the West. It was a job equal to the building of a Pyramid and it may be considered as an effort whose significance was on a par with the invention of the printing press. On the day when more Liberty ships were built than Allied ships were sunk by the Germans, we can say that day was the turning point of the war. The shipbuilding effort was for the construction of 2,700 Liberty ships. The Liberty ship WISTERIA, illustrated above, had been converted from an ordinary cargo ship to a hospital ship.

The steamer was launched as the WILLIAM MOSLER at the shipyard of the Ellicott Machine Corporation, Baltimore, MD. The ship's 7,940 gross tonnage included all the upperworks added into the calculations. The Liberty ships built in the United States during World War II had an aggregate tonnage greater than three times the tonnage of all the ships in the American Merchant Marine at the beginning of the war. One Liberty ship was built, as a publicity stunt, in four days. What a shock this demonstration must have been to the top officials in Nazi Germany. When first projected, the Liberty was called an "Ugly Duckling" by President Franklin D. Roosevelt. Little did he realize what an impact this one project would have on world history.

The American Merchant Marine Museum held a reunion in 1988 for seamen who served on Liberty ships in the war. With little publicity for the event, more than 400 people arrived. One of the museum's choice artifacts is a 15-foot long model of a Liberty ship, the prototype model built by Higgins Shipyard, New Orleans, LA. It was presented in 1942 to the United States Merchant Marine Academy by President Roosevelt and used to train Merchant Marine officers for the war effort. The ship's hull is made of transparent plastic and each rib is visible to familiarize young officers with every location on the ship. In case of a fire or torpedo explosion the midshipman would be able to shout out the number of the rib nearest to the accident.

The most famous name in the Liberty shipbuilding effort was Henry J. Kaiser, West Coast industrialist whose several shipyards produced hundreds of Liberty ships. The official Maritime Commission designation for the Liberty ship was E (for Emergency) C (for Cargo) 2 (for bigger than 1)-EC2.

Publisher: Western Cruise Lines, Miami, FL • Manufacturer: Dynacolor Graphics, Inc., Miami, FL • Type: Color Glossy Photograph • Postmark: Not Used • Value Index: E

Publisher: United States Navy Military Sea Transportation Service • Manufacturer: Hanover Enterprises,Inc., 545-5 Fifth Avenue, New York, NY • Type: Colored Glossy Photograph • Postmark: Not Used • Value Index: E

This liner began life in 1944 as the *GENERAL W.P. RICHARDSON*, a P-2 type troopship built at the Federal SB & DD Company Yard, Kearny, NJ. The ship remains in service at this writing as a cruise ship known as the *EMERALD SEAS*, as shown in this illustration. She was originally named after a West Point graduate, Wilds Preston Richardson, a member of the class of 1884 who fought in the Apache Indian War. Five different ship lines purchased and rebuilt the ship after the liner's period as a troopship. Initially, the steamer was rebuilt by American Export Lines to operate as the *LA GUARDIA* for trips to the Mediterranean. Then the *LA GUARDIA* was purchased for operation between California and Hawaii in American flag cruise service and renamed *LAILANI* (meaning "Lively Flower"). Problems with food poisoning and flooded cabins due to a hasty refitting operation badly damaged the ship's reputation. The American President Lines purchased the *LAILANI*, rebuilt the steamer from bow to stern, spending $8,000,000 in the effort, and renamed the ship *PRESIDENT ROOSEVELT*. However, rising costs doomed the ship operations to failure and the new purchaser was the Chandris Line, well-known for using second-or-third-hand ships. The ship was again renamed, *ATLANTIS*. The rebuilding was more costly than the previous $8,000,000 reconstruction. Years passed and the *ATLANTIS* was purchased by the *Eastern Steamship Lines*. More rebuilding followed and the name *EMERALD SEAS*. With a limited capacity of 960 passengers and a crew of 360 people the veteran liner had at long last found a formula for success. The ship was able to operate at a 14-knot speed and make money. Her dimensions were: length 622 feet, beam 76 feet, 12,400-mile radius. The *EMERALD SEAS* is currently owned by the Admiral Line, a part of the Royal Caribbean Line combine.

1936 Merchant Marine Act, known as the "Magna Carta" of the American Merchant Marine, provided a framework for the revival of America's merchant fleet after the Economic Depression. Under the able direction of Joseph Kennedy, father of the late President, a new shipbuilding program was begun. More ships were constructed during this effort than at any other time in the history of the world. More than 5,000 merchant ships were built, of which the largest single group were the 2,700 Liberty ships. The P-2 Troopship Building Program was the climax of this plan. Most of the ships laid down were completed in time for World War II service. Two shipyards produced all the P-2 transports: the Bethlehem SB Corporation, Alameda, CA, which built the Admiral Class, and the Federal SB & DD Company, Kearny, NJ where the Generals were built. The Generals were slightly larger than the Admirals.

This illustration shows the *ADMIRAL W.S. SIMMS* and it represents the ships of the West Coast. There were eight Admiral Class P-2s. Their dimensions: 17,000 gross tons, 609 feet in length, 75-foot beam, turbo-electric propulsion with a 19-knot speed, 15,000-mile radius, wartime troop capacity 4,971, and cargo capacity 36,720 cubic feet. Ten vessels had been contracted to be built, but the end of the war halted the completion of the last two ships as troopers. They were acquired by American President Lines and finished as trans-Pacific passenger liners.

The *ADMIRAL W.S. SIMMS* was named after the Commander of United States Naval Forces in European waters during World War I. The ship was rebuilt almost as soon as she left the shipyard. The *SIMMS* was used in 1946 to carry Army troops and their dependents to and from overseas stations. In 1948 the transport was renamed for a young American Ranger leader killed in the Italian Campaign, becoming the *GENERAL WILLIAM O. DARBY*.

In 1950 the vessel was rebuilt to serve the United States Navy with a crew of 294 civilians and 26 naval personnel, a troop capacity of 1,307, and cabin facilities for 250 adults, 181 children or 132 infants. As time passed the work for moving troops was given to the Military Sea Transportation Service (MSTS). Greater care was given to make the ships more attractive. Eventually, aircraft supplanted the ships for all troop movements and the P-2s were laid up.

The *AQUARAMA* was a wartime cargo ship of the C-4 type. These ships had their engines aft as they had been designed to carry long pieces of lumber from the Pacific Northwest. She was originally named the *MARINE STAR* one of five special C-4s built in 1945 by the Sun SB & DD Company, Chester, PA. The dimensions: 520 feet long, 72 feet wide, geared turbine propulsion with a single propeller, and 19-knot speed. Many of the C-4s became wartime troopships while others were rebuilt as hospital ships. In 1952 the ship was acquired by *Sand Products Corporation* of Detroit, MI. The ship was brought to Todd Shipyards Brooklyn, NY plant where all of the erections higher than 55 feet were cut off and stowed on deck to permit passage under Mississippi and Illinois Waterway bridges. The ship was to become a luxurious passenger excursion boat for the Great Lakes. The plan was to introduce an ultrastreamlined passenger ship for daily round trips between Detroit, MI and Cleveland, OH. The steamer in this illustration was renamed *AQUARAMA*. She is now owned by the Michigan-Ohio Navigation Company and there are hopes that this veteran will again see active service on the Great Lakes.

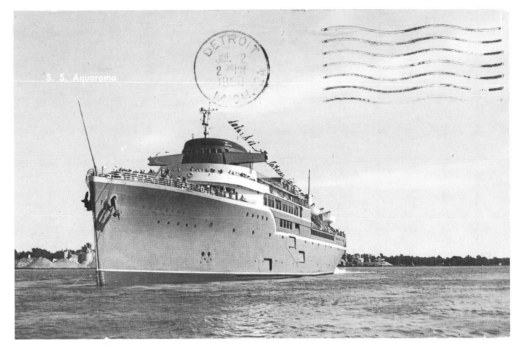

Publisher: Plastichrome by Colourpicture Publishers, Inc., Boston, MA • Manufacturer: Hiawatha Card of Detroit, P.O. Box 488, Ypsilanti, MI • Type: Colored Glossy Photograph • Postmark: Sea Cliff, NY, July 5, 1960 • Value

Second to the Liberty ship program was the Victory ship. Nearly 600 of these much faster cargo ships were built in the latter days of the war when victory was assured. They were much more expensive than Liberty ships, required more time to build, and lasted longer. Many were converted for other uses, including passenger ships such as the *WOOSTER VICTORY*, and the Spanish luxury liner *MONSTERRAT*. The ship was built in 1945 by the California SB Corporation, Los

Publisher: Compania Trasatlantica Espanola • Manufacturer: Estades-Madrid, Spain • Type: Colored Glossy Painting • Postmark: Not Used • Value Index: D

Angeles, CA. This steamer was one of 97 Victory ships converted to troopships during the war. At the end of the war the greatest ship sale program of all time began with the United States Government offering thousands of surplus merchant ships to American companies, then opening the sale to foreign nations. The Societa Italiana Trasporti, Geono, Italy, known as the Sitmar Line, purchased the *WOOSTER VICTORY* for their immigrant run from Italy to Australia. The ship was rebuilt, and renamed *CASTLE VERDE*. Finally, the ship was sold to a Spanish line.

The *EXETER* shown in this illustration was the third of four passenger-cargo ships ordered by the American Export Line to replace the original "Four Aces." These vessels were the new "Four Aces." All four were rushed to completion in 1945 for service in World War II. In 1948 they were rebuilt as originally planned. The sea trials for the *EXETER* were held on November 3, 1948. This initial cruise occurred on Election Day, when everyone anticipated that Republican Thomas E. Dewey would defeat Harry S. Truman for the Presidency. Everything went as expected through the morning and afternoon

American Export Lines' New "4 Aces"— S.S. EXCAMBION, S.S. EXOCHORDA, S.S. EXETER, S.S. EXCALIBUR

Publisher: American Export Lines • Manufacturer: Harry H. Baumann, New York, NY • Type: Colored Dull Finish Photograph • Postmark: Not Used • Value Index: E

tests at sea. However, in the evening news surprising election trends indicated Truman upset Dewey.Many of the reporters had filed colums for the next day's newspaper based on a landslide for Dewey. The last hours of the ship trial were hopeless for the American Export publicity people as none of the reporters appeared to care about the ship. The *EXETER* was the *SHELBY*, APA 105 in the war, and was built at the Bethlehem Steel Sparrows Point, MD shipyard.The *EXETER* and the *EXCALIBUR* were sold in 1965 to C.Y. Tung for his Orient Overseas Line, renamed *ORIENTAL PEARL* and *ORIENTAL JADE*, and operated for some time across the Pacific Ocean. When this company went bankrupt following the death of Tung, Sr., the ships were scrapped.

The country's first luxury liner built since World War II was launched January 11, 1946 at the Pascagoula, MS yard of the Ingalls Shipbuilding Corporation. The ship built for the Delta Line was named *DEL NORTE*, and was the first of three 10,073-gross-ton ships. The trio of ships were of all welded construction.The two other ships that were built were named *DEL MAR* and *DEL SUD*. Contemporary reports described the "Huge Tear-Shaped Stackhouse" as the most outstanding feature of the liner. It was constructed of aluminum and weighed nearly 75,000 pounds, representing a saving of approximately the same

Delta Line REGULAR SCHEDULES BETWEEN U. S. GULF PORTS AND - BRAZIL URUGUAY ARGENTINA WEST AFRICA

Publisher: Delta Line • Manufacturer: Sutherlin Sales Company, New Orleans, LA • Type: Colored Glossy Photograph • Postmark: Not Used • Value Index: E

amount of weight in displacement. The smoke from the boilers was carried high off the decks by two king post-like pipes that came through the after edge of the stackhouse and rose above it. The *DEL NORTE* was believed to be the first ship of this class to have only lower berths. All staterooms for the 121 passengers were air conditioned. A crew of 124 persons made for a passenger crew ratio more favorable than the most luxurious of traditional liners. After short careers the trio was sold for scrap in 1972.

Three American passenger ships built on Victory ship hulls, owned by the Alcoa Steamship Company and named *ALCOA CAVALIER, ALCOA CLIPPER,* and *ALCOA CORSAIR.* The ships were built at the Oregon SB Corporation, Portland, OR. The price per ship was $3,800,000. George Sharp was the naval architect for the conversion to passenger ship work. The steamers had initially been designed as cargo ships, then as 50-passenger combination liners, and finally as luxury one-class ships for 98 passengers. The dimensions were, 8,481 gross tons, 445 feet in length, a beam of 63 feet, 8,500 horsepower with

Publisher: Alcoa Steamship Company • Manufacturer: Not Indicated • Type: Black-White Dull Finish Photograph • Postmark: Not Used • Value Index: E

a single propeller. The ships were capable of a 17-knot speed. There were 95 crew members. Aluminum was used for the officer's deck house, the bridge, smokestack, and all of the structure above the sun deck. A large quantity of aluminum was used for interior furniture, fittings, and trim. By 1960, after only 13 years of use, the service was discontinued.

The last two P-2 troopship hulls were not completed as planned. They were sold to the American President Lines and finished as luxury liners *PRESIDENT CLEVELAND* and *PRESIDENT WILSON* for trans-Pacific service. Had these ships been completed during warime, they would have been called the *ADMIRAL D.W. TAYLOR* and the *ADMIRAL F.B. UPHAM,* respectively. The measurements were 15,456 gross tonnage, 609 feet long, 76 feet wide, with turbo-electric, twin screw propulsion, 19-knot speed, fully air conditioned. They were the first major postwar liners built in America.

Two overhauls in 1960 and again in 1963 brought them up to the highest stan-

Publisher: American President Lines • Manufacturer: Not Indicated • Type: Colored Glossy Painting • Postmark: Not Used • Value Index: E

dards for liners. This illustration shows a decidedly glorified artistic conception of the *PRESIDENT WILSON.* As an example, a typical itinerary required that the ship: leave San Francisco, CA on December 27 and return on February 9. For two decades the liners were popular and profitable. Then they were withdrawn and sold to C.Y. Tung's Oriental Overseas Line, becoming the *ORIENTAL PRESIDENT* (ex-*CLEVELAND*) and *ORIENTAL EMPRESS* (ex-*WILSON*). High fuel prices prevented their use and they were sold for scrap, the *CLEVELAND* in 1975 and the *WILSON* in 1985.

This illustration shows two famous American liners. To the left is the *FRANCA "C"* (which began life in 1914 as the *MEDINA*) and to the right the *INDEPENDENCE*. The ships are anchored at a pier in Gibraltar. The *INDEPENDENCE* and the sistership *CONSTITUTION* are still sailing under the American flag at this writing. When launched at the Bethlehem Steel Company's Quincy, MA shipyard on June 3, 1950. Both vessels are well maintained and

Publisher: Rock Photographic Services, Gibraltar, Card No. Legal R. 11836-1964 • Manufacturer: Not Indicated • Type:

operated under the American flag. Their dimensions make them the third and fourth largest passenger ships to fly the flag of the United States. The 30,293 gross ton (British measurement) ships are now operated by American Hawaii Cruises. Both ships were given an added deck in 1959 in a most unusual operation. The forepart of the superstructure was lifted up the height of one deck and moved 22 feet forward. The empty space was filled with new cabins and passenger facilities.

To this day the *UNITED STATES* remains the greatest, safest, and fastest passenger ship ever built in the United States and perhaps, the world. William Francis Gibbs, the naval architect-marine engineer, made this ship his lifelong project. He succeeded in producing a ship which has never been equaled in massive appearance, power, and innovative style. The story begins in 1916 when Gibbs sold his idea to J.P. Morgan. For the next three decades whenever any of his staff had a free moment Gibbs would put him to work on "The Big Ship," which broke all Atlantic Ocean speed records on her first trip in

Publisher: United States Lines • Manufacturer: Richkrome-Exclusively by Steelograph Company, One Broadway, New York, NY • Type: Colored Glossy Photograph • Postmark: Not Used • Value Index: F

1952. Gibbs had top secrecy as he was certain the enemy (British shipowners) were spying.. A comment as written in the British humor magazine Punch. It said, in effect, that after all the noise and blare from America about the new superliner's features, it is most awkward to have to admit that every claim made is true. However, there was a weakness in the fact that the ship was completed too late.. Competition from the jet airliner destroyed the basis for the success of the new superliner. In 1969, a year after Gibbs had passed away the ship was laid up in Norfolk, VA.

The cargo liner *BADGER MARINER* was converted into a passenger ship. This Mariner class of ships was a new type cargo vessel and were the first to be government-sponsored since World War II. Completed in 1953 this vessel was 564 feet long, 76 feet wide, and was built by Sun SB & DD Chester, PA. The conversion into a 14,136-ton passenger ship in 1956 was accomplished at the Ingalls Shipbuilding Company, Pascagoula, MS. Renamed *ALTANTIC* this ship was the climax to a career for shipowner Arnold Bernstein. He was

Publisher: Postales Escudo De Oro-Ediciones Barcelona, Spain • Manufacturer: A Subirats Casanovas, Valencia, Spain • Type: Colored Glossy Photograph • Postmark: Not Used • Value Index: D

faced with problems: competitors, not obtaining a good Hudson River pier, and continuing to make changes in the rebuilding specifications. The line was called the American Banner Line, with AB on the stack. The company was short lived. The ship was purchased by the American Export Lines (AEL). The *ATLANTIC* did well, however, the AEL was bought by the Isbrandtsen Lines when it expanded and became a victim of poor management. In 1971 C.Y. Tung bought the ship to have a floating university. The *UNIVERSE CAMPUS*. The name was shortened to *UNIVERSE* and the floating university has continued in operation. She is registered in Liberia and is operated by World Explorer Cruises, of San Francisco, CA.

Two rebuilt Mariner cargo ships emerged as the Matson Line's *MONTEREY* and *MARIPOSA*. They were the first American liners to be equipped with the Sperry Gyro Stabilizers. A small ship, with only one propeller they had more vibration than a ship with twin screws. Their contract speed was 20 knots and on the trials the *MARIPOSA* did 24.6 knots. The *MONTEREY*, originally *FREE STATE MARINER*, was built in 1953 by Bethlehem at their Quincy, MA yard. The *MARIPOSA* (ex-*PINE TREE MARINER*) was built at the Bethlehem Sparrows Point, MD.

Publisher: Matson Lines, Card No. 8202 • Manufacturer: Not Indicated, Litho in USA • Type: Colored Glossy Photograph • Postmark: Not Used • Value Index: F

Another ship, built for the Grace Line, which has suffered neglect for many years is the *SANTA ROSA*. Designed by William Gibbs, she was a high point in passenger comfort for cruise ships. The Grace Line was restive, moving ahead on other fronts and losing interest in shipping. On the March 26,1959, a major collision occurred and the *SANTA ROSA* was only slightly damaged. She entered New York City Harbor bearing the smokestack of the tanker *VALCHEM* on her bow. Four crewmen on the tanker were killed and one on the *SANTA ROSA* suffered a fatal heart attack. Several of the 247 passengers aboard were

Publisher: F.A. Russo, Inc., 230 Park Avenue, New York, NY, Card No. 10385-B • Manufacturer: K.N., Inc. • Type: Colored Glossy Painting • Postmark: Not Used • Value Index: F

slightly injured. Photographs of the new Grace Line flagship coming into port with the huge stack of the tanker in a prominent position at the tip of the bow caused the company to be embarrassed. Repairs were quickly made to the *SANTA ROSA* and on April 16, 1959 the liner was ready to return to service. The Grace Line sold their marine operations to the Prudential Lines and the *SANTA ROSA* was laid up in Baltimore, MD late in 1978. On December 19, 1989, the liner was taken under tow for Greece.The ship had been sold at auction for $3,000,000 to be rebuilt at the cost of $80,000,000 as a cruise ship. The rebuilt ship's name will be *DIAMOND ISLAND*.

Albert V. Moore and his partner Emmet J. McCormack sat in their Moore McCormack Lines private office one day in the middle 1950s. They told the author, "We are designing two new ships right now." These ships became the *ARGENTINA* and the *BRASIL* and the ships were constructed by the Ingalls SB Corporation, Pascagoula, MS. The *ARGENTINA* entered into service December 19, 1958, followed shortly in the same year by the *BRASIL*. The *ARGENTINA* is now known as the *BERMUDA STAR*, and was the *MONARCH STAR*, and *VEENDAM*. The *BRASIL* is known as the *QUEEN OF BERMUDA*, having sailed also as the *LIBERTE*, *MONARCH SUN*, and

Publisher: Bermuda Star Line • Maufacturer: Not Indicated • Type: Colored Glossy Photograph • Postmark: No Postmark, Canadian Postage Stamp, Postcard was written August 9, 1988 • Value Index: E

VOLENDAM. These ships measured 15,257 gross tons when new, increased to 20,614 gross tons when they were enlarged in 1963, and currently are 23,500 gross tons using British tonnage rules. They are 617 feet long and 86 feet wide. Each ship cost $26,000,000 and could carry 663 passengers when rebuilt. As Mormac Liners they sailed from New York City. With geared turbines, 17,500 horsepower, and twin screws at 21 knots.

Publisher: American Export Isbrandtsen Lines • Manufacturer: Not Indicated • Type: Colored Glossy Photograph • Postmark: Not Used • Value Index: E

Imagine a ship important enough to have the Vice President's wife officiate at the keel laying and the President's wife do the honors at the launching. The ship was the first of its type and was hailed around the world as the pioneer of the greatest step in maritime evolution since steam won out against sail. Then the ship became involved in worldwide denunciation, an invitation to the worst possible labor problems, and the subject of an intra-union battle which caused all operations to be stopped for more than a year. Finally, all of the high ideals that were originally integral to the use of the ship were forgotten and the whole effort was allowed to appear as a complete failure when the government made the ship into an ordinary cargo vessel. This story relates to the *SAVANNAH*, the world's first nuclear powered passenger-cargo ship.

The entire effort involving much high idealism, hope, and work is almost forgotten. It was a dream of President Dwight D. Eisenhower and his hope was to show that America wished to use atoms for peace and everything about the *SAVANNAH* was to be open for study and observation by anyone from any land. Mrs. Richard Nixon officiated at the keel laying on May 22, 1958. It was suggested that this date be chosen as it was the anniversary of the sailing of the first *SAVANNAH*, built in 1819, the first ship with a steam engine to cross any ocean. Mrs. Eisenhower christened the ship on July 2, 1959. The *SAVANNAH* was to sail the seven seas to preach the message of using atoms for peace. There would be space aboard for 60 passengers, with luxurious cabins and elegant public rooms. A worldwide sailing schedule was worked out with rates for short and long trips to large and small ports on every continent. Foreign political and social leaders were to be entertained on trips or as guests for goodwill dinners aboard in the principle ports. However, as soon as President Eisenhower was out of office these high goals began to change. At the same time an unexpectedly powerful antagonism to atomic power, both in America and abroad, caused a wave of opposition to the ship. Many ports refused to permit the *SAVANNAH* to visit. Then labor problems arose. The only way to solve the crisis was to let everyone go, and all of people who had trained for this new challenge were dismissed.

A new union, which included every rating from Master to ordinary seaman, from Chief Engineer to wiper, was founded in the Brotherhood of Marine Officers. They provided the new crew and finally *SAVANNAH* was able to sail again. The States Marine Lines, which had been the agent for the ship earlier, had to be dropped, and the American Export Lines took over the assignment. The ship ran for several years, losing money continually, although American Export was asked to pay only the most nominal charter hire. All the pomp was gone and only the headaches remained. The *SAVANNAH* was quietly laid up and forgotten. Today if you ask anyone about this ship and you will get a blank stare. The whole matter has passed into limbo.

The *SAVANNAH* measured 13,599 gross tons, was 595 feet long, 78 feet wide, had a single screw and could make 21-plus knots. New York Shipbuilding Corporation, Camden, NJ were the builders. The first atomic core used to power the *SAVANNAH* drove the ship for 332,405 nautical miles. In the ship's total steaming of nearly half a million miles, approximately 163 pounds of nuclear uranium fuel were used. In five years of operation the ship visited 77 ports in the United States and 25 foreign countries, was visited by about 1,250,000 people, and carried 154,000 tons of cargo. The *SAVANNAH* is now an exhibit at the Maritime Museum in Charleston, SC.

The four *SANTA MAGDALENA* class ships came out of the Bethlehem Sparrows Point, MD shipyard in 1963 and 1964 with an ultramodern silhouette and without a smokestack. The smoke came out of a tall pipe just aft of a flat, raised, and rounded deck house, which included bridge and officers quarters. In Grace Line Press releases Fred Sands, public relations director for the company, had named it the "Smoke Stalk." Later, Sands announced a decision to install real smokestacks to end the negative publicity their stackless liners had earned. The new smokestacks were built and lifted aboard by helicopter. They were small and did

Publisher: Foto Flatau, Apartado 391, Panama,R.P., Card No. C18145 • Manufacturer: Mike Roberts Color Productions, Emeryville, CA • Type: Color Glossy Photograph • Postmark: Not Used • Value Index: E

not have the proper appearance. These liners were elegant passenger-cargo vessels, perhaps the finest built at that time. The other ships were named *SANTA MARIANA*, *SANTA MARIA*, and *SANTA MERCEDES*. The four ships were dedicated to four Central American countries the Grace Line originally intended to serve. This quartet could carry 175 20-foot containers. Each had four traveling gantry cranes for loading and unloading and had the capacity to carry 90,000 stems of bananas. Three ships were sold for scrap in 1988 and the *SANTA MERCEDES* was rebuilt for service as a merchant marine officer training ship.

The *CAPTAIN PATTERSON* is 75 feet long, 18 feet in beam, and has a draft of approximately four feet. The vessel is powered by three Detroit Diesel engines, with three shafts and propellers. Using the two decks, the ship can carry 300 passengers on the route linking Bay Shore and Kismet, NY. The ship is the first steel-hulled ferry specially designed for Great South Bay Ferry Service. The concept was the work of Captain Elmer Patterson; he was founder of Fire Island Ferries. The ship was built by Blount Marine, of RI, required five months to build, and entered service in mid-May, 1972. At this writing, the craft has made more than 10,000 round trips to Fire Island.

Publisher: Fire Island Ferries, Inc., Photograph by Frank Mina • Manufacturer: Tomlin Art Company, Box 93, Islip, NY • Type: Colored Glossy Photograph • Postmark: Not Used • Value Index: F

This photograph is of an American built and operated passenger ferry *M.V. COLUMBIA*. The plans for this ship werer prepared in 1971 by Philip E. Spaulding & Associates. The projected cost was $18,800,000. The diesel-powered vessel was operated by the Alaska Marine Highway System, with headquarters in Juneau, AK. The construction costs were higher than anticipated, and a number of features were eliminated why no new passenger ships are being built in the United States. The *M.V. COLUMBIA* was launched in

Publisher: C.P. Johnston Company, Seattle, WA, Photograph by Max R. Jensen • Manufacturer: Mike Roberts Color Productions, Emeryville, CA • Type: Colored Glossy Photograph • Postmark: Not Used • Value Index: F

1973 by the Lockhead Shipbuilding Company of Seattle, WA. In 1990 the vessel was shifted to begin the run from the new terminal in Bellingham, WA. When the *COLUMBIA* entered the Alaska Marine Highway System, the new vessel was designated fleet flagship. The dimensions: 3,946 gross tons, 418 feet in length, 85 feet beam, and 12,350 horsepower. The motor ship had a cruising speed of 17.3 knots and a fuel consumption of 750 gallons per hour. At this writing, the service has nine vessels and covers 2,000 miles as America's largest ferry system.

The *MISSISSIPPI QUEEN* was built in 1975, with a gala christening at Louisville, KY. The builders Jeffboat, Inc., of Jeffersonville, IN, are the source of the *ROBT E. LEE II* and the *J.M. WHITE,* and more than 4,800 steamboats in the 19th century. None could compare to the $27,000,000 *MISSISSIPPI QUEEN*. The 4,500-gross-ton steamboat, three times the size of the *DELTA QUEEN*, has a length of 382 feet, 67-foot beam, and draws 8.5 feet of water. The ship's top deck is 52 feet above the water. The 80-ton crimson stern wheel is pushed by eccentric pitman arms weighing 20 tons. The engines were made by the Marietta Manufacturing Company, Point Pleasant, WV.

MISSISSIPPI QUEEN

Publisher:Delta Queen Steamboat Company, New Orleans, LA, Photograph by R. Michael Ricouard • Manufacturer: Express Publishing Company, New Orleans, LA • Type: Colored Glossy Photograph • Postmark: Not Used • Value Index: F

Barnie Ebsworth is founder of the Clipper Cruise Line. He was a catalyst in the creation of the Royal Cruise Line. In the 1980s he helped create one of the first successful new coastal passenger ship lines. To date, the company has built three small passenger ships: *NEWPORT CLIPPER* in 1983, *NANTUCKET CLIPPER* in 1985, and *YORKTOWN CLIPPER* in 1988. The first two ships (*NEWPORT CLIPPER* and *NAN-*

Clipper Cruise Line • Manufacturer: Not Indicated • Type: Colored Glossy Photograph • Postmark: Not Used •Value Index: F

TUCKET CLIPPER) are identical sisters, each 207 feet long, 37 feet wide,   carrying 102 passengers with a crew of 28, and costing $10,000,000. Both have a technical 99.5 gross tons (The "technical"means very little, but permits the smaller ships to operate under somewhat more lenient Coast Guard rules) The ships were constructed by Jeffboat, Inc., Jeffersonville, IN. The *YORKTOWN CLIPPER* has a length of 251 feet and can accommodate 138 passengers.

The *CARIBBEAN PRINCE* is another coastal passenger vessel with an American flag and crew. Captain Luther H. Blount, President of Blount Marine Corporation was the builder-operator of this ship. The ship was Hull No. 250 for Blount Marine Corporation. The motor vessel was launched on October 25, 1983 and put into service on December 4, 1983. Their earlier ship is currently on coastal routes under the Blount-owned American Canadian Caribbean Line is the *NEW SHORE-HAM II*. Both ships feature the bow landing ramp, a lightweight aluminum gangway, which Blount invented, to be

Publisher: Luther H. Blount, Blount Marine, Warren, RI • Manufacturer: LK Color Productions, P.O. Box 6262, Providence, RI • Type: Colored Glossy Photograph • Postmark: Not Used • Value Index: F

placed into position at an open door in the ship's stem. Passengers walk on this gangway and on land. The *NEW SHOREHAM II*, Blount's Hull No. 225, was launched on September 21, 1979 and delivered November 18, 1979. The original *NEW SHOREHAM* has been renamed *GLACIER BAY EXPLORER*. This craft, new in 1971, was Blount's Hull No. 153. The *CARIBBEAN PRINCE* is 165 feet long and has a beam of 65 feet. A crew and staff of 19 people are required. He builds his ships to travel under the many low bridges on this historic waterway from Waterford, NY to Owsego, NY and Lake Ontario. The stack and rails are constructed to fold down. The pilot house sinks down into a space on the deck below.

Publisher: American Cruise Lines • Manufacturer: SSD-MWM Dexter, Aurora, MO • Type: Colored Glossy
Photograph • Postmark: Not Used • Value Index: F

Publisher: Manhattan Post Card Publishing Company, Inc., Glendale, NY, Card No. WB656, Photograph by Bart Barlow •
Manufacturer: Kina, Milan, Italy • Type: Colored Glossy Photograph • Postmark: Not Used • Value Index: F

American Cruise Line offered hope of a substantial revival for American passenger shipping when it was formed in the 1970s. The company went into bankruptcy late in 1988 and its ships are still laid up at Haddam, CT. Showing remarkable initiative the company had a shipyard in Salisbury, CT on the eastern shore of Maryland, where it built several steamers, starting with the *AMERICA* in 1982. Earlier ships of the American Cruise Line fleet included the 60-passenger *AMERICAN EAGLE*, the 81-passenger *INDEPENDENCE*, the 90-passenger *AMERICA*, and then came the *SAVANNAH, NEW ORLEANS*, and *CHARLESTON*. The *NEW ORLEANS*, shown in this illustration, was larger than all the other ships in this fleet and was intended for use on the Mississippi and Ohio rivers.

The company made a custom of selling the smallest vessel in their fleet each time they built a new one. American crews were employed. The *NEW ORLEANS* was designed using traditional Mississippi riverboat lines and this steamboat entered service in the summer of 1985. To quote from one of the company's advertisements the new river steamer has "The opulence of another age." Described as a floating luxury hotel, "Shining brass and richly textured woods in the new vessel." The *NEW ORLEANS* has four passenger decks.

The South Street Seaport Museum operates two diesel-driven replica steamboats for New York City harbor excursions. The Seaport Line project began in 1984 when Brian McAllister, President of McAllister Bros. Towing Company, one of New York's two major tug companies, called William H. Muller, noted marine artist who had specialized in Hudson River type steamboats. McAllister asked Muller to "Undertake the project of designing the `Look' of the proposed boats." As a result of this initiative, two of the finest old-style craft in the world operate out of South Street, Pier 167, East River, NY.

The first of these working excursion boats is a sidewheeler *ANDREW FLETCHER*, named after the port's famous engine builder. The second ship is the *DE WITT CLINTON*. The *FLETCHER* dimensions: 125 feet in length and 46 feet in beam. With three decks this vessel can accommodate 400 passengers. The *FLETCHER* entered service in 1985, was successful, and prompted an order for a second ship. The 150-foot long, 600-passenger *DE WITT CLINTON*, is propeller driven, was put into service in 1986. Both ships were built by the Offshore Shipbuilding, Inc. of Palatka, FL in 1989. The American Merchant Marine Museum presented plaques in 1989 to Brian McAllister, William H. Muller, and Seaport President Peter Neill for their important contribution to life in New York made more enjoyable by these two replica steamboats.

Publisher: Coastwise Cruise Line, Photograph by Douglas Alvord • Manufacturer: Not Indicated • Type: Colored Glossy Painting • Postmark: Not Used • Value Index: C

This replica ship *PILGRIM BELLE* was built in 1984. The ship was ordered by Coastwise Cruise Line, of Hyannis, MA. The ship is smaller with the outline and style of past Long Island Sound steamers. The builder was Bender Shipbuilding & Repair Company, Inc., Mobile, AL. The diesel powered 110-passenger ship was designed by John W. Gilbert & Associates in Boston, MA. Dimensions are 192 feet long, 40 feet wide, and 300 horsepower. For added maneuverability the *PILGRIM BELLE* was equipped with a bow thruster.

During the delivery voyage the new ship made a stop at the New York City South Street Seaport Museum. Two months later the craft ran aground in Buzzards Bay, MA while on a week-long cruise in southern New England. The 84 passengers aboard were all rescued, with five people treated for shock at a Falmouth, MA hospital. Although there was a 3 x 6 foot-hole in the hull the ship did not sink. The Coastwise Cruise Line went out of business.

The vessel was sold to the Exploration Cruise Lines and renamed *COLONIAL EXPLORER*. In 1989, when this company collapsed, the ship was idle on the West Coast. She was then chartered as a dormitory by the Exxon Company, for people hired to clean up the Alaskan oil spill from the tanker *EXXON VALDEZ*. When this work ended for 1989, the *COLONIAL EXPLORER* was acquired by the St. Lawrence Cruise Lines of Kingston, Ontario, Canada, a new company with one small ship, the *CANADIAN EXPRESS*, operating between Kingston and Quebec City, Canada. They renamed the ex-*PILGRIM BELLE* the *VICTORIAN EMPRESS*.

BIBLIOGRAPHY

The following books and publications were used as sources of information in preparing this book:

Adams, Arthur G., *THE HUDSON THROUGH THE YEARS*, Lind Publications, Westwood, NJ, 1983

Anderson, Elizabeth Stanton, *COASTAL STEAM VESSELS*, Meriden Gravure Co., Meriden, CT, 1960

Angas, W. Mac. Commander, *RIVALRY ON THE ATLANTIC*, Lee Furman,Inc., 1939

Blum, Ethel, *THE TOTAL TRAVELER BY SHIP, 1985-1986* Edition, Travel Publications, Inc., Hippocrene Books, NY

Bonsor, N.R.P., *NORTH AMERICAN SEAWAY*, Five Volumes, Arco Publishing Co., NY 1975 (New edition)

Bowen, Dana Thomas, *LORE OF THE LAKES*, Dana Thomas Bowen Publisher, Daytona Beach, FL, 1940

Bowen, Dana Thomas, *MEMORIES OF THE LAKES*, Dana Thomas Bowen Publisher, Daytona Beach, FL, 1946

Braynard, Frank O., *A TUGMAN'S SKETCHBOOK*, John de Graff, Inc., Tuckahoe, NY, 1965

Braynard, Frank O., FAMOUS AMERICAN SHIPS, Hastings House, NY, 1978 (New and revised edition)

Braynard, Frank O. and William H. Miller, *FIFTY FAMOUS LINERS*, Patrick Stephens, Ltd., Wellingborough, UK, 1982-87, Volumes I, II, III

Braynard, Frank O., *LEVIATHAN, WORLDS' GREATEST SHIP*, Privately Printed, 1972-83, Volumes I, II, III, IV, V, VI

Braynard, Frank O., *LIVES OF THE LINERS*, Cornell Maritime Press,Cambridge, MD, 1947

Braynard, Frank O., *S.S. SAVANNAH, THE ELEGANT STEAM SHIP*, University of Georgia Press, Athens, GA, 1963

Brown, Alexander Crosby, *THE GOOD SHIPS OF NEWPORT NEWS*, Tidewater Publishers, Cambridge, MD, 1976

Brown, Giles T., *SHIPS THAT SAIL NO MORE*, University of Kentucky Press, 1966

Cairis, Nicholas T., *CRUISE SHIPS OF THE WORLD*, Pegasus Books, Ltd., London, UK, 1988

Charles, Roland W., *TROOPSHIPS OF WORLD WAR II*, Army Transportation Association, Washington, DC., 1947

Cram, W. Bartlett, PICTURE HISTORY OF NEW ENGLAND PASSENGER VESSELS, Burntcoat Corporation, Hampden Highlands, ME, 1980

Dayton, Fred Erving, *STEAMBOAT DAYS*, Frederick A. Stokes Company, NY, 1925

Deland, Antoinette, *FIELDING'S WOLRDWIDE GUIDE TO CRUISES*, William Morrow & Company, NY, 1981

Dunn, Lawrence, *PASSENGER LINERS*, Adlard Coles, Ltd., London, UK, 1965 (Revised edition)

Fahey, James C., *FAHEY'S 2ND WAR EDITION-THE SHIPS & AIRCRAFT OF THE U. S. FLEET*, Ships and Aircraft, 1265 Broadway, NY, 1944

Fairburn, William Armstrong, *MERCHANT SAIL*, Fairburn Marine Education Foundation, Inc., Center Lovell, ME, 1945-55

Flexner, James Thomas, *STEAMBOATS COME TRUE*, Viking Press, NY, 1944

Gibbs, C.R. Vernon, Commander, *BRITISH PASSENGER LINERS OF FIVE OCEANS*, Putnam, London, UK, 1957 (2nd edition)

McAdam, Roger Williams, *COMMONWEALTH-GIANTESS OF THE SOUND*, Stephen Daye Press, NY, 1959

McAdam, Roger Williams, *PRISCILLA OF FALL RIVER*, Stephen Daye Press, NY, 1947

McAdam, Roger Williams, *SALTS OF THE SOUND*, Stephen Daye Press, NY, 1939 (Reprinted 1957)

McAdam, Roger Williams, *THE OLD FALL RIVER LINE*, Stephen Daye Press, NY, 1937 (Reprinted 1955)

McDonald, Lucile, *ALASKA STEAM*, A Pictorial History of the Alaska Steamship Company, Alaska, Geographic, Edmonds, WA

Melville, John H., *THE GREAT WHITE FLEET*, Vantage Press, NY, 1976

Miller, William H., Jr., OCEAN LINERS OF THE WORLD, Quadrant Press, Inc., NY, 1984

Newport News Shipbuilding and Dry Dock Co., *THREE GENERATIONS OF SHIPBUILDING*, Privately Printed, Newport News, VA, 1961

Niven, John, *THE AMERICAN PRESIDENT LINES AND ITS FOREBEARS 1848-1984*, University of Delaware Press, Newark, 1987

Ringwald, Donald C., *HUDSON RIVER DAY LINE*, Howell-North Books, Berkeley, CA, 1965

Smith, Eugene W., *PASSENGER SHIPS OF THE WORLD, PAST AND PRESENT*, George H. Dean Co., Boston, MA, 1963

Sniffen, Harold S., *ANTONIA JACOBSEN- THE CHECK LIST,PAINTINGS & SKETCHES BY ANTONIO N.G. JACOBSEN-1850-1921*, Sanford & Smith Galleries, Ltd., NY and the Mariners' Museum, Newport News, VA, 1984

Stadum, Lloyd M., *DENALI WAS A GOOD INVESTMENT, THE SEA CHEST*, Puget Sound Maritime Historical Society, 1985

Stanton, Samuel Ward, *AMERICAN STEAM VESSELS*, Smith & Staton, NY, 1895

Steamship Historical Society of America, *MERCHANT STEAM VESSELS OF THE UNITED STATES 1807-1868*, The Lytle List, Publication No. 6, Mystic, CT, 1952

Stindt, Fred A., *MATSON'S CENTURY OF SHIPS*, Privately Printed, Matson Navigation Co., Kelseyville, CA

MAGAZINES:

Marine Engineering & The Log, Various issues

Ocean Ferry, International Mercantile Marine, NY, Various issues

Sea Breezes Liverpool, UK, Various Issues

Steamboat Bill, Steamship Historical Society of America

INDEX

NOTES

NOTES

NOTES

NOTES

NOTES